Spiritual

MW01121898

The
Basics
Of
Prayer

An In-Depth teaching on

The Lord's Prayer

By Kenneth Scott

Scriptures in this publication are taken from the King James version of the Bible and paraphrased by the author.

The Basics of Prayer
Printing 06010 OP

ISBN: 978-0-9667009-8-5

Contents

Preface

For centuries, churches, as well as individuals have adopted "The Lord's Prayer" as the prayer in which we are to pray each day. You can hardly find anyone that prays at all who doesn't know the Lord's Prayer. Most Christians know the Lord's Prayer verbatim. For many, along with the 23rd psalm, it's the only passage in the Bible they know. We have passed it down from generation to generation, teaching our children that this is the prayer that Jesus taught us to pray. Many Christians are diligent to pray or quote this passage on a daily basis. However, many who pray or quote it, do so without understanding the meaning of the words and phrases in this passage. Proverbs 4:7 reads, "*...with all thy getting get [an] understanding.*" In other words, God is saying, don't just learn His Word, or learn to pray or quote it from memory, get an understanding (from God) of what His Word is truly saying. This book was written to help give the believer an in-depth understanding of the Lord's Prayer.

Isaiah 28:10 instructs us to learn the Word of God, "*line upon line, precept upon precept; here a little, and there a little.*" This is how we have broken down this passage. I have taken each section and broken it down so that you may better understand the Lord's instructions in this passage, and thereby learn how to pray more effectively. If we are going to use this passage as a pattern of prayer, we must get an understanding of that pattern.

In the military you have two areas of training before you are ready for war. You have what is called basic training (also called "BT"), and you also have what is called advanced individual training (also called AIT). Basic training teaches the soldier the basic necessities of war. It teaches the soldier the proper attitude, discipline, and mentality a soldier needs to fight on the battlefield. It teaches the soldier how to fight and survive using the basic weapons and tactics of combat. AIT goes beyond basic training and teaches the soldier advanced tactics and combat skills, as well as gives them advanced knowledge on specialized equipment and weaponry in their particular field. If they could, most soldiers would prefer to skip basic training and go directly to their advanced portion of training. However, all solders must go through basic training before they can go on to other more advanced training.

The Lord's Prayer is a type of basic training of prayer. Before you can go on to your spiritual AIT of supplication, intercession and other mature areas and levels of prayer, you must first get an understanding in, and become versed and disciplined in prayer in the areas taught in the Lord's Prayer. Once you gain an understanding of the Lord's Prayer, and become disciplined in prayer in these areas, you will then be ready for your spiritual AIT, and ready to become more effective in your next level of warfare.

Introduction

Some people actually think that the Lord's Prayer is the only prayer that we are to pray each day. So they get on their knees each morning and spend all of 30 seconds out of their day praying this prayer. The Lord's Prayer was the first prayer Jesus taught His disciples, but it was not the only one. There are many principles of prayer that Jesus taught throughout the gospels. There were also many other principles and instructions on prayer taught throughout the New Testament by the disciples and apostles, as well as by other men of God in the Old Testament.

It's like the 10 Commandments. Many regard the 10 Commandments as the entire compass of God's laws. The 10 Commandments were only one set of laws in which God gave His people to follow after He delivered them from Egyptian bondage. When God tells us to do something, it is not a suggestion, but a commandment. God has given us many instructions of things we should do as well as things we should not do. Each time we fail in either of these areas, we break the commandment of God. From Genesis to Revelation there are many commandments in which God has given us. In the same manner, the Lord's Prayer was not the only time that God gave His people instructions on prayer. There were many instructions on prayer given in the Old Testament. There were also many prayers in which Jesus prayed in the New Testament. The Lord's Prayer is simply one of them. But again, it's the basics of what you need to pray.

> *And it came to pass, that, as He was praying in a certain place, when He ceased, one of His disciples said unto Him, Lord, teach us to pray, as John also taught His disciples.*
>
> *Luke 11:1*

The Lord's Prayer is actually an outline of prayer. It is an outline of things we should pray for or pray about on a daily basis. It also teaches the proper attitude we should have concerning prayer. Jesus did not intend for this to be the limit of our prayer. Instead, it was only meant to be the beginning.

The above verse is another account of the same passage (of the Lord's Prayer). If you notice, the disciples asked Jesus to teach them how to pray. First of all, they asked Him to teach them how to pray because they really didn't know how to pray. They knew the ritualistic patterns of prayer they were taught to pray. And, they knew how to cry out to God and tell Him what was on their hearts. But they noticed something different about Jesus' prayers from their own, and from the prayers their religious leaders prayed.

They noticed that His prayers were not just empty, vain words spoken simply to fulfill a daily duty of prayer. They noticed that His prayers were strategic and full of power and authority. And last, they also noticed how effective His prayers were. Now even though they knew how to pray (according to the Jewish laws, customs, and traditions), compared to Jesus, they realized that they really didn't know how to pray at all.

Let me say first of all that the Lord's Prayer should not be the sole prayer for the mature Christian. Again, the Lord's Prayer is only an outline of things that we should pray for each day. This is where we began in prayer each day. If you were to give instructions to a child, you would try to make your instructions as simplistic as possible. After that child began to learn, you would then begin to give more complicated instructions on that particular subject or item. At this point, the disciples were spiritual children. Because they were, Jesus did not use the Lord's Prayer as an advance or complex instruction on prayer, but like you would do a child. He instructed them in a simplistic, elementary manner. As they continued to walk with Christ, they saw Him praying about other things. And although the Bible does not note it, it is assumed that they eventually learned more about prayer.

This book, *"The Basics of Prayer"* helps to give the believer an understanding on the basic principles of prayer in which Jesus taught His disciples. They are basic principles of prayer that most Christians think they know, but many really don't know.

Chapter 1

The Preliminaries of Prayer

Private Prayer Before Public Prayer

And when thou prayest, thou shalt not be as the hypocrites are: for they love to pray standing in the synagogues and in the corners of the streets, that they may be seen of men. Verily I say unto you, they have their reward.

Matthew 6:5

Before Jesus began teaching the disciples about the Lord's Prayer, He began giving them preliminary instructions about prayer. In verse 5, He began talking about the motive of prayer. He instructed them to not be like the hypocrites (referring to the Pharisees) who loved praying in public places to impress people and show off what they thought was their spiritual superiority. Jesus said that they were nothing but hypocrites.

There are many people who (like these Pharisees) love to get in church, bible studies, and around other people and pray. Although what they are doing may be good, the motive behind what they do is wrong. Their motive is simply to impress others. Jesus was not teaching that it is wrong for us to pray in public, but to make sure that our motive is right when we pray in public. The hypocrisy Jesus was referring to was the fact that these Pharisees prayed dramatically in public, but at the same time probably had little or no prayer life at home.

Prayer is a reflection of your relationship and intimacy with God. And, if you don't have a private relationship and intimacy with God (by spending quality time with Him each day in prayer and worship), it is hypocrisy to get in public and attempt to pray (trying to make others believe that you have been with God), when in fact you have not. It's equivalent to a man that is married, who, while at home doesn't spend time talking with his wife or being affectionate to her at all. But when he gets around his friends, church members, and others, he puts on a display by opening the door for her, speaking gently and kind to her, and showing her affection. If anyone really knew this man, and how he truly treated his wife at home, they would call this man a hypocrite. This is the same reason why Jesus called these Pharisees hypocrites. If this man in our example treated his wife the same at home as he did in public, he could not be called a hypocrite. In the same manner, when we pray at home the way we do in public, God will likewise not look upon us as hypocrites.

Then they took away the stone from the place where the dead was laid. And Jesus lifted up His eyes, and said, Father, I thank thee that thou hast heard me. And I knew that thou hearest me always: but because of the people which stand by I said it, that they may believe that thou hast sent me. And when He thus had spoken, He cried with a loud voice, Lazarus, come forth.

John 11:41-43

The above passage is part of the account of Jesus raising Lazarus from the dead. If you notice, before Jesus raised Lazarus from the dead, He prayed to the Father saying, "*I thank thee that thou hast heard me,*" meaning, in His private prayer time. Jesus was able to do this, as well as other miracles in public because of what He did in private. It's in your private prayer time with God that you get His presence, anointing and power to be able to pray for others and demonstrate the power of God when you need to pray in public. Make sure that before you pray in public that you get alone with God in private. Because, it's in your private time that you get what you need from God to be able to demonstrate His power in public.

A Time To Pray

But thou, <u>when thou prayest</u>, enter into thy closet, and when thou hast shut thy door, pray to thy Father which is in secret; and thy Father which seeth in secret shall reward thee openly.

Matthew 6:6

The first emphasis I would like to bring out in this passage is, "*when thou prayest...,*" meaning, that you need to have a time to pray. We have a specific time to be at work in the morning. We have a specific time to be at church. We have specific times to be at most places and events we attend, so we need to also have a specific time for prayer. Have you ever heard of an event in which people were instructed to come whatever time they decided to come? If that were so, you wouldn't have many people to attend that event. Most important events require you to be at a specific place at a specific time. Likewise, you need to have a specific time of prayer.

> *Now Peter and John went up together into the temple at the <u>hour of prayer</u>, being the ninth hour.*
> *Acts 3:1*

If you are going to be effective in prayer, you must develop a time for prayer. Most people who are not disciplined to have a time for prayer usually wake up in the morning and take care of their particular duties or agenda first (such as preparing themselves for work and preparing the kids for school), and then, whatever time they have left, they give to prayer. When you do not set a time for prayer, the devil will make sure that something comes up that takes away most of your time for prayer—leaving you only a few moments to pray, if any time at all. For people with this type of morning routine, prayer is not a priority for them. They take care of their priorities first, and then take care of prayer last. When prayer is a priority, you will set a time to pray first, as well as set a time for your other morning duties and preparations.

Set yourself a time for prayer that allows you to be able to spend an hour, or at least 45 minutes in prayer and devotion with God before you begin your other daily duties. If you have children, make sure that this time is before your children wake up. If you allow your prayer and devotion time to be during the time your children are awake, the devil can easily use them to constantly interrupt and distract you. If you somehow wake up late in the morning, purpose in your heart to set your lunchtime, or your first legitimate break time as your time to pray. Don't wait until you get home in the evening to pray. By that time you will be both physically and mentally tired. When you set yourself a time in the morning to pray, you will become a disciplined soldier of Christ and keep the devil from robbing you of your prayer time, and thereby keep him from hindering your day or even your life.

A Place To Pray

But thou, when thou prayest, <u>enter into thy closet.</u>

Matthew 6:6

In the above passage, this closet that Jesus makes reference to is not a literal closet, but a spiritual one. Everyone needs a prayer closet. Your prayer closet is simply a place where you can get alone with God by yourself and talk to Him. Your prayer closet can be your living room, bedroom, kitchen, porch, or any place you can get alone and be open and honest with God in prayer.

Shut The Door

But thou, when thou prayest, enter into thy closet, <u>and when thou hast shut thy door</u>, pray to thy Father which is in secret...   —*Matthew 6:6*

While rooms in your home may serve as your normal closet for praying for things that may be somewhat common, general or non-sensitive, there will be times in your life where you may need to go to what I call "an outward closet." I believe that this is what Jesus meant when He said to "**shut the door**." Although you can shut the door inside your home by getting alone in a place by yourself and pray quietly to God, there will be times in your life when you will need that door shut, as the saying goes, "tight as a drum." In other words, you will need to find a place where no one can hear you at all. There will be times that you will need to literally cry out to God about sensitive, personal issues in your life. In these times, rooms in your home may not be private enough, and you may need to go for a walk, or even go for a drive in your car.

When I pray, I am somewhat loud. Most of the time I am comfortable walking through my home praying, or kneeling praying in my living room. But in the times when I need to cry out to the Lord about something heavy upon my heart, or pray about something personal or sensitive, I go for a walk down a particular seldom traveled road about 3 miles in distance. There are few cars that pass down this road. I'm out there by myself with no one else around me, giving me the opportunity to cry out to the Lord like I need to do.

I'm out there with my hands lifted up to God — sometimes literally crying. Sometimes I even kneel on the side of the road in the dirt and pray. I'm sure that the people in the few cars that pass by wonder if I have lost my mind. To them it probably looks like I'm talking to myself in some kind of rage or emotional despair. I have had people to stop me and ask me if I was all right. Although they can see me, they can't hear me, which allows me the privacy to express myself to God the way I need to.

There are other times I go for a drive in my car and find a place that is somewhat secluded and park and do the same. Other times I drive down a road where there is not much traffic. This is not an everyday experience for me, but I do it as I need to. Your closet can be somewhere different every day. The place that you make your closet (whether it's an in-home closet our outward closet) is not as important as the principle of both having and utilizing it.

Vain Repetitions

But when ye pray, use not vain repetitions, as the heathen do: for they think that they shall be heard for their much speaking.

Matthew 6:7

I have had many people to call and tell me that they could not pray from my book (*The Weapons of Our Warfare*) because they read that we are not to pray vain repetitions. When people tell me that, I always inform them of the fact that when Jesus said for us not to pray vain repetitions, it wasn't the repetitious part of praying that He was referring to, but the part about the prayers being vain.

In Luke 18:1-7 there is a parable Jesus gave about a widow woman who wanted justice. It notes that she came over and over again asking for justice for the same thing. Finally, because of her persistence, she received justice. This parable was a symbol of prayer—teaching us about the reward of persistent prayer. However, in the midst of her persistence, she continued to come over and over again with the same request. Jesus didn't say anything derogatory about her repetitious requests. In fact, it was her persistent, repetitious requests that enabled her to receive justice, which simply symbolizes answered prayer. Likewise, there is nothing wrong with you praying a repetitious prayer, as long as it is not a vain repetitious prayer. Again, the emphasis here is on the prayer being vain, not repetitious.

What Is A Vain Prayer?

There are three things that make a prayer vain. One aspect of a vain prayer is the scripture passage we covered in our last point.

1. Hypocrisy

And when thou prayest, thou shalt not be as the hypocrites are: for they love to pray standing in the synagogues and in the corners of the streets, that they may be seen of men. **—Matthew 6:5**

These hypocrites that Jesus is referring to are people who love to pray while they are in church, or around others, but do not have the same heart and passion for prayer at home. Jesus went on to say that they already have their reward (the praise of men). In other words, God will not answer their prayers. It's not a vain prayer because they prayed in public, but because of their prideful motive to impress others and show off through the vehicle of prayer. So whenever a prayer is prayed in public with the intent to show off and impress, and not a reflection of the type of prayer life they have at home, the prayer is a vain prayer.

2. Prayers Without Honesty and Humility

A second aspect of praying a vain prayer is praying a prayer that is not from the heart, and is prayed without truth, honesty and humility before God.

Two men went up into the temple to pray; the one a Pharisee, and the other a publican. The Pharisee stood and prayed thus with himself, God, I thank thee, that I am not as other men are, extortioners, unjust, adulterers, or even as this publican. I fast twice in the week, I give tithes of all that I possess. And the publican, standing afar off, would not lift up so much as his eyes unto heaven, but smote upon his breast, saying, God be merciful to me a sinner. I tell you, this man went down to his house justified rather than the other...

Luke 18:10-14

In the above passage, you find two men praying. Although both men prayed, the Pharisee's prayer was based on his good merits, and his attempt to exalt himself before God, while at the same time looking down at the publican. On the other hand, the publican (who was despised and looked down upon by the Jewish people) came to God in prayer openly and honestly before Him. He didn't try to justify himself before God. He wasn't trying to impress anyone around him. Neither did he try to exalt himself before God in his own self-exalted righteousness. Jesus said, this man (the publican) went home justified (having his prayers answered) and the Pharisee did not. In this parable, the Pharisee prayed a vain prayer because the intentions, motive, and attitude of his heart toward God, as well as the publican were wrong.

When you come to God in prayer, you must humble your heart before Him as this publican did. You have to leave behind your accomplishments of who you are in the community and who you are in the church, as well as your degrees, positions, and titles. The Pharisee was a religious leader equivalent in our day to a priest, pastor or minister. First, he thought that his position as a religious leader gave him credence with God. Secondly, he thought that his good works and merits gave him credence with God.

When you come before God in prayer, you must not only humble your heart before Him, but you must also come knowing that nothing you have and nothing you've done merits you any special credit with Him. It doesn't matter whether you are the holiest person in the church or the most sinful person in the church. Neither does it matter whether you are the pastor or lay member, or whether you are the richest or poorest; you must still come before Him in the same way. If you are saved, you must come with the attitude knowing that you are only saved by the grace of God and the blood of Jesus Christ.

Even though you may be a good person and may serve the Lord diligently within and outside the church as well, you still have no place to stick your chest out to God in pride. Your good works do not merit you any special position with God.

I'm not saying that we should not do good works before God. If you are saved and born again, you should serve Him and do good works. However, they don't gain you any special place with Him. The revelation of a difference is this: We do what we do good works because we love Him, and not because we are trying to earn a special place with Him. Any prayer that is prayed with self-exalted pride in your position or accomplishments is a vain prayer.

3. Prayers With No Substance

The third part or aspect of a vain prayer is one that is prayed without the substance of God's Word. For years, we have been taught that when we pray, we should just say what's on our hearts. There are times in which we pray that we need to cry out to the Lord from our hearts, such as in the prayer or cry of repentance or special supplication. However, God has given us directives by which to pray.

> *... ye have not, because ye ask not. Ye ask, and receive not, because ye ask amiss...*
>
> *James 4:2-3*

Praying "amiss" is to pray the wrong way. One of the errors (amiss) of praying and petitioning God is when we pray without using the substance of His Word. In the above passage God is saying that this is one of the reasons why we *"have not"* (do not get our prayers answered) when we pray.

> *Put me in remembrance: let us plead together: declare thou, that thou mayest be justified.*
>
> *Isaiah 43:26*

In this passage God instructs us to put Him in remembrance. He is referring to the remembrance of His Word. It's not that God cannot remember what He has said and needs us to remind Him, but He is trying to teach us a principle of prayer. Our words by themselves have no power. But when we come to God and begin to pray His Word, it has power, and God brings His Words to pass. God honors His Word, not ours. And, when we pray and speak His Word, He honors it and brings it to pass. Don't try to move God in your emotions, bring His Word to Him. And, when you do, He will honor "His" Word and bring it to pass.

O Israel, return unto the LORD thy God; for thou hast fallen by thine iniquity. <u>Take with you Words</u>, and turn to the LORD: say unto Him, Take away all iniquity, and receive us graciously: so will we render the calves of our lips.

Hosea 14:1-2

In this passage, God gives us instructions of how to come before Him in prayer. He says that when we come before Him to bring "**Words**" with us. He is not talking about our plain words of what we think or feel, but rather, His Words (the Word of God). When you come before God with a petition, you must find His Word that corresponds with your need or desire, and petition Him based upon what His Word says about your request.

For example: If you have a need for finances, you would need to find a scripture such as Philippians 4:19, which says, "*But my God shall supply all your need according to His riches in glory by Christ Jesus.*" You would then take that Word and apply it personally to your life and make your petition to God based upon that Word. You would then pray, "**Father, I thank you for the promise of Your Word to supply all of my needs according to Your riches in glory. I thank You therefore for meeting my financial need according to Your Word.**"

Bless the LORD, ye His angels, that excel in strength, that do His commandments, hearkening unto <u>the voice of His Word</u>.

Psalms 103:20

The above passage tells us that angels go forth to carry out the voice of God. The voice of God is His Word. When you pray His Word, the angels of God have permission from God to move out and carry out the Word of God that you pray and confess.

The above passages all represent the fact that when we pray and petition God, we must come before Him utilizing His Word, rather than what we think or feel. So again, a vain repetition is not a prayer that is prayed repeatedly, but rather, one in which is prayed in one of the three following facets:

1. With the intent to show off or to impress others.
2. With pride or self-exaltation because of works, a title or position.
3. Without the substance of using the Word of God in your petition.

Chapter 2

Our Father Which Art In Heaven

After this manner therefore pray ye: Our Father which art in heaven, Hallowed be thy name. Thy kingdom come. Thy will be done in earth, as it is in heaven. Give us this day our daily bread. And forgive us our debts, as we forgive our debtors. And lead us not into temptation, but deliver us from evil: For thine is the kingdom, and the power, and the glory, forever. Amen.

Matthew 6:9-13

When Jesus introduced God as Father, He was introducing God to them in a way in which they had never known Him. In the past, they had come to know God as Jehovah. They knew Him as Jehovah Jirah, Jehovah Raphi, Jehovah Nissi, and other names. Jehovah simply means God, or "God is." The rest of the name is what God became to them in a particular situation. For example: If they sought the Lord for healing, and the Lord healed them, they would call God Jehovah Raphi, meaning, the Lord God my healer. If they had a particular need, and the Lord provided for them, they would call Him Jehovah Jirah, meaning, the Lord my provider. If they needed peace in the midst of trouble or turmoil, they would call Him Jehovah Shalom, meaning, the Lord my peace.

Another way they came to know the Lord was through the names of their founding fathers. They knew Him as the God of Abraham, Isaac and of Jacob. The reason why they would address God in this manner is that God made a covenant with Abraham, Isaac and Jacob to bless them and their descendents. So when they addressed God in this manner, they were identifying themselves as descendents of Abraham, Isaac and Jacob, and therefore part of the covenant blessings which God had made with them.

There are many people in the world now who still believe that the Jews (descendents of Abraham) are the only ones who can inherit the blessing of the Lord, as well as receive eternal life in glory. There is a degree of truth about this statement. However, the blessings of God are not reserved for the physical descendents of Abraham. Instead, they are reserved for the spiritual children of Abraham.

> *Know ye therefore that they which are of faith, the same are the children of Abraham.*
> *Galatians 3:7*
> *And if ye be Christ's, then are ye Abraham's seed, and heirs according to the promise.*
> *Galatians 3:29*

The promises of God and inheritance of eternal life are not reserved for the physical Jews, but for those who are the spiritual seed and descendents of Abraham. When you receive Christ, you are spiritually adopted into the family of God, and through the covenant that God made with Abraham and his seed, you are also able to receive the blessings of God upon your life.

> *They answered and said unto him, Abraham is our father. Jesus saith unto them, if ye were Abraham's children, ye would do the works of Abraham...Jesus said unto them, If God were your Father, ye would love me: for I proceeded forth and came from God; neither came I of myself, but He sent me...Ye are of your father the devil, and the lusts of your father ye will do...*
>
> John 8:39, 42, 44

The above passage is an account of an encounter Jesus had with the Pharisees. They boasted in the fact that they were descendents of Abraham. Jesus informed them that even though they were physical descendents of Abraham, that because of their sinful works and rejection of Him (Christ), instead of Abraham being their father, the devil was their true father instead. When we receive Christ and walk in His ways, we become the (spiritual) seed of Abraham even though we are not (physically) Jews.

Being a spiritual Jew now gives us the privilege of addressing God as "Our Father." It's like a child having a friend whose father was rich. Let's say this child's name is Michael, and his friend's name is Larry Jones. Whenever this child would go over his friend's house, he would have to address his friend's father as Mr. Jones. Whenever he would make reference to Mr. Jones, he would have to refer to him either as Larry's Father or Mr. Jones. But let's say that Mr. Jones adopted Michael. Once the adoption was complete, he would no longer need to refer to him as Mr. Jones. He would now be able to refer to him as "My Father," or if talking to Larry, "Our Father."

This is what has happened to us in the spiritual realm. Through Christ, God has now adopted us into the family of God. And because we are adopted, we now have the right to boldly come before Him as "Our Father." Now, even though God was their Father through the covenant He made with Abraham, Isaac and Jacob, God had never revealed Himself to them in this manner before.

Jesus now comes on the scene and introduces God to them in this manner. One of the reasons why God had not introduced Himself to them as "Father" was because of sin. Sin kept God from having an intimate relationship and fellowship with man prior to the coming of Christ. Even though they made sacrifices (in the Old Testament) for their sins, the sacrifices of animals and birds could only hide their sins; they could not eradicate their sins completely because the sacrifices themselves were imperfect.

When Jesus came, He came as the complete, perfect and eternal sacrifice for man. When Jesus introduced God to them as "Father," He was introducing God to them based upon the fact that He (Jesus) was to die for the sins of man, completely eradicating man's sins, thereby allowing man an opportunity to have intimate fellowship with Him once again. I say once again because Adam once had intimate fellowship with God. But after sin entered in, the fellowship was severed. But when Jesus completed His task of dying on the cross, His blood erased our sins, and thereby reestablished our ability to have intimate fellowship with God once again. So again, when Jesus introduced God to them as "Our Father," He was showing them that God was now ready (through the blood of Christ) to have intimate fellowship with man once again.

Daddy God

There is a big difference between knowing God as the God of the universe, and knowing God as your Heavenly Father. When you truly come to know God as your Heavenly Father, you too will come to not only know Him as the creator of the universe, but also as the God who is full of mercy, love, and grace.

> *And He said, <u>Abba, Father,</u> all things are possible unto thee; take away this cup from me: nevertheless not what I will, but what thou wilt.*
>
> *Mark 14:36*

> *For ye have not received the spirit of bondage again to fear; but ye have received the Spirit of adoption, whereby we cry, <u>Abba, Father.</u>*
>
> *Romans 8:15*

In this first passage here in Mark 14:36, Jesus refers to God as *"Abba Father."* Abba means "daddy." So in essence Jesus was calling God, "Daddy God." In the second passage in Romans 8:15, Paul, speaking to the church, also refers to God as "Abba Father."

Knowing God as "Daddy," brings us to a new understanding and dimension of intimacy with God. There is a difference between a man being a father and being a daddy. A father is simply a man who is biologically able to produce seed and bring forth a child. It doesn't take anything special to be a father. A man doesn't have to have any character or good traits to be a father. To be someone's father, all he has to do is be able to produce good seed. However, it takes much more to be a daddy. I myself, like many others had a (biological) father, but never knew him as "daddy." To be a daddy takes love, mercy, compassion, care, concern and many other good attributes.

"Daddy God" also expresses another side of God. It is the mothering side of God. Parental figures of both the father and mother are represented in God as "Our Father." It has been said that the love of a mother is the closest we will ever get on earth to understanding God's love for us. There is an unconditional love that a mother has for her child. This love is not predicated upon how good or bad that child may be. It's unconditional.

When Jesus revealed God as "Our Father," He was not only revealing the awesomeness of God as the creator and ruler of the universe with all power, dominion and authority, He was also revealing both parenting sides of God. He was revealing the "Daddy" side of God, which is one of provisions, safety, kindness, comfort and strength for us. And, He was also revealing the "Mothering" side of God, which is one of caring, mercy, compassion and unconditional love for us.

What this should do for us regarding prayer is to help us come to God in a different manner. If a child has a daddy (and or mother), that child knows that it doesn't matter what the have done in the past, how bad they have messed up, or how bad they've been; they know that they can still come to their parent(s) and know in confidence that their parent(s) will still love them no matter what. A daddy (and or mother) may not like all the things their children do, but it never stops the parent(s) from loving them, caring for them, and taking the time to listen to and comfort them no matter what they've done.

You may or may not have had good earthly parents. Your parents may even be deceased. But if you would come to know God as "Our Father," you will find that He is the perfect parent that will listen to you, encourage, strengthen, comfort, and love you unconditionally.

Come Boldly Before Him

When we approach God in prayer, many times we approach Him with feelings of being unworthy and with feelings that God will not hear our prayers based upon our sins or wrongdoing. But you need to understand that God has adopted you into the family of God and has become your "Abba Father."

> *Let us therefore come boldly unto the throne of grace, that we may obtain mercy, and find grace to help in time of need.*
>
> *Hebrews 4:16*

In the book, *"The Weapons of Our Warfare,"* I begin most of the prayers with the above scripture by praying in this manner: **"Father, I come boldly before Your throne of grace...."** The reason I begin most prayers this way is to help the one praying to have the right attitude when coming before God in prayer. No matter how bad you've sinned, what you've done, or how bad you have missed it with God, you still have the right to boldly come before Him in prayer. Remember, God sent His Son to die on the cross for our sins, iniquities, and transgressions. It was God's love for us (**For God so loved the world...**) that He, as our loving, caring, compassionate Heavenly Father, sent His only begotten Son into the world to die on the cross for the sins of man. The blood of Jesus Christ gives you the right to boldly come before God. What you have to understand about God is that His love for you through Christ Jesus is far greater than all the sins or wrongdoings you have done or could ever do. As long as you come before God with a humble and repentant heart, you can boldly come before Him knowing that (through Christ) you have been adopted by God as one of His children, and therefore have the right to boldly come before Him in prayer.

Many people come before God feeling unworthy to face Him in prayer. I've heard many people begin their prayer like this: **Father, creator of the universe, your unworthy servant comes before you in prayer. I know that I am not worthy of your grace, and not worthy to come to you to-day, but I come as humble as I know how in prayer....**

If you are not born again, this may be the way you need to pray (because you are not worthy without Christ and His precious blood). However, if you are born again, then you are worthy to come before Him because Christ has made you worthy. If you are born again, God not only wants you to come to know Him as the God of the universe, but also as "Daddy God," the one who loves you, cares for you, and the one who is compassionately waiting for you to come to Him. And, the one who loves you so much that He sent Jesus to die on the cross for your sins, iniquities and transgressions so that you can boldly come before Him in prayer.

Although we may be unworthy (because of our sins), we are made worthy through Jesus Christ to come boldly before Him. And, as long as we are willing to come before Him in honesty and truth, like a daddy, He is willing to listen to whatever our needs are with compassion, kindness, and His love.

This first part of our prayer, ***"Our Father which are in heaven,"*** reflects both how we address God and the attitude in which we are to come before Him in prayer.

Chapter 3

Hallowed Be
Thy Name

Praying Through the Name of
Jesus Christ

W hen we approach God in prayer, the first thing we do is address God as, "Our Father" or "Heavenly Father." We must approach Him with the right attitude of Him not only as being the God of the universe, but also our intimate, loving, compassionate Father. *"Hallowed be thy name"* has a two-fold meaning. As we mentioned earlier, our adoption into the family of God is through the blood of Jesus Christ.

It is His blood that validates us, justifies us, and redeems us. It is also through His blood that we are forgiven of our sins, accepted by God, and can boldly come before the throne of God in prayer. Without Jesus, there is no redemption, reconciliation or forgiveness of sins. Without

Him, man would be alienated from God. It's like God being on one side of a steep cliff and man being on the other side. Jesus Christ became the bridge between God and man. However, in order to get to the other side, you must go across the bridge. Jesus Christ, and His precious name is the bridge that links us to The Father. Without Him, and without His name, there is no access to God.

> *Jesus saith unto him, I am the way, the truth, and the life: no man cometh unto the Father, but by me.*
>
> *John 14:6*

> *Neither is there salvation in any other: for there is none other name under heaven given among men, whereby we must be saved.*
>
> *Acts 4:12*

Among the many complaints that other religions, doctrines and beliefs have about Christians, one of the biggest is that they say we are too narrow-minded. They say that we should be more open and willing to receive other beliefs and religions as another way in which we can get to God. We are narrow-minded, and should be. When we stand before God to be judged, we will be judged by one of two standards: We will either be judged according to our sins, or according to our acceptance of Christ.

If we have accepted and received Christ, we will stand blameless of sin and worthy to enter into the Kingdom of heaven. We will not be worthy to enter in by our works of righteousness, but by the righteousness and blood of Jesus Christ. However, if we have not accepted and received Jesus Christ, we will be judged according to our sins. And, if we must be judged according to our sins, we are already guilty. So yes, we are narrow-minded, but we should be because we are "only" saved by Jesus Christ.

Not only do we have salvation through the name and blood of Jesus Christ, our access to God and to His blessings also come through His name. One of the above passages tells us that we cannot even get to God (in prayer) without coming through Jesus Christ. In Chapter I (Vain Repetitions) we brought out three things that make our prayers vain. If we included this point in that section, it would make it number four, because when we pray and do not come through the name of Jesus Christ, it is a vain prayer and God will not hear it. Because, once again, Jesus Christ and His precious name is the bridge, and without the bridge, there is no access to God. Therefore, either at the beginning of your prayer or at the end of your prayer, you must validate that prayer with God through the name of Jesus Christ.

You can either begin your prayer with the name of Jesus Christ, or you can end it with the name of Jesus Christ. If you begin it with His name, you can begin like this: **"Father, in the name of Jesus Christ I come boldly before you in prayer…."** If you choose to end your prayer with His name, you can end it the way I end most of my prayers. In our prayer handbooks we end all of our prayers with, **"In the name of Jesus Christ, I pray, AMEN."** Either way is correct, just as long as you use His name.

Christ the Anointed One

And Simon Peter answered and said, Thou art the Christ, the Son of the living God.

Matthew 16:16

Prior to the above passage, Jesus had asked His disciples whom did men say that He was. They first gave several names referring to Jesus as Old Testament prophets. But then Peter boldly spoke up and said, *"You are the Christ, the Son of the living God."* It wasn't enough to simply know Him as Jesus. The revelation came in knowing Him not only as Jesus, but also as "Christ." There is something significant about using the name Jesus and Christ together.

The meaning of the name of "Jesus" is "Savior." The meaning of "Christ" is "the Anointed One." And when you refer to Jesus as Christ, you're calling Him, "the Anointed Savior." There are many people living in our day with the name of Jesus. I saw a baseball player with the name Jesus. I have seen people who have named their children Jesus. Although there are many people in our day named Jesus, there's only one Jesus who is the Christ, the Anointed one. So when you pray, don't just come to God in the name of Jesus, come also with Christ, the Anointed One. I'm not saying that it would be incorrect to say Jesus only, but what I am saying is that there is something powerful about the name, "Jesus Christ." So when you are dealing with the devil, don't just cast him out in the name of Jesus alone; he may think you are talking about the name of someone named Jesus who has no power. Go ahead and cast him out in the name in which he will have no doubt by whom you are speaking; cast him out in the name of Jesus Christ. And, when you come to God in prayer, come also in the powerful and awesome name of Jesus Christ.

Worship, Praise and Thanksgiving

The word *"Hallowed"* means holy, reverence, or sacred. The first part of "*Hallowed be thy name*" refers to the way we validate our prayer through the name of Jesus Christ. The next part of "Hallowed be thy name" refers to the reverence, honor, and worship we should give to Him when we approach Him in prayer.

In the Old Testament there were three sections to the tabernacle. There was the outer court, the inner court, and the most holy place (also called "the holy of holies"). The outer court is where the common people would assemble, pray, and worship God. The priests however, were the only ones who could come into the inner court. But only the high priest could come into the holy of holies. This was a physical place that represented the presence of God. It was in the inner court that the priest communed with God and made sacrifices to Him on behalf of the people.

I. Procedures to See the King

These three courts also represent how we approach the throne of God in prayer. It also represents how people would approach a king in the days of old. In those days you didn't just walk up and begin talking with the king. You had to follow proper protocol and procedures if you wanted to see the king. You would first have to ask for permission to speak with the king. Sometimes your appointment to see the king could take days, weeks or even months. If you were granted permission to see him, you would then be given a particular day and time. It was customary that if you had an appointment with the king to come and wait for him early in the morning. Although he may not have even begun seeing people until the afternoon, it was respectful to the king for you to come early in the morning.

There were two reasons for coming in early to see the king. One reason was that in case the king's earlier appointments went faster than anticipated, you could be available to come in earlier for your appointment. The second reason was because it was considered disrespectful for the king to wait for anyone. It was much more respectful for you to come in hours earlier to wait for the king, than for the king to wait for you one moment. If you came in at the last minute for your appointment, even though the king may not have asked for you yet, it was considered disrespectful to the king, and you would often be denied permission to see him. However, if you came early in the morning and waited for him, it was seen to be respectful, and that you were giving honor and respect to the king.

Once you arrived for your appointment to see the king, you would wait in a waiting area called the outer court. This was an informal waiting area where people would wait for their time to see the king. Once the king gave permission for you to see him, your name would be announced, and you would be escorted inside into the inner court, also called the king's hall.

Once you entered into the inner court, you would come up to a certain point and stop. It's at this point you would kneel before the king, and wait for the king to give you permission to rise and come closer. Failure to stop at this point and give the king proper respect and reverence by bowing or kneeling before Him would be seen as disrespectful. And, depending on how the king interpreted or viewed this level of disrespect, you could either be denied permission to speak to him, or even placed in prison. In some extremes cases you could even be executed. Once the king had a look at you and wanted to speak with you, He would either nod his head or stick out his scepter—giving you permission to come closer.

Once you were given permission to come closer, you would then be escorted to the edge of the king's throne area. This area was usually about twenty feet from where the king sat. It was close enough for the king to clearly see and converse with you, and yet far enough away where the guards could quickly respond in case you tried to harm him. Once you approached this area, you would once again either kneel or bow before the king. Once he gave you permission to rise and speak, you would begin by magnifying the king in some type of salutation. The salutation would have to be something that exalted the king, such as, *"May the king live forever"* or, *"May all the king's enemies be destroyed."*

After your salutation, you would then thank the king for honoring you and allowing you to come before his presence to speak to him. After that, you would then present your petition. Once again, failure to follow these procedures to the letter in properly approaching the king could result in the person being denied permission to speak to him, being jailed, or in some cases, executed.

II. The Proper Protocol of Worship

> *Enter into His gates with thanksgiving, and into*
> *His courts with praise: be thankful unto Him, and*
> *bless His name.*   *—Psalms 100:4*

In prayer, it is also important how we approach "The King." Just as there was proper protocol in which a person had to approach a king in ancient days, this passage also shows us a parallel in how we approach our King in prayer. Many people are ineffective in prayer because they do not know how to properly enter into the presence of God. Just as improperly approaching a king in days of old could result in the person being denied permission to see the king, if you improperly approach "The King" (the throne of God), it could result in your request being denied, or death to your petition.

The second part of *"Hallowed be thy name"* represents the worship, praise and exaltation we are to give God when we enter into prayer. Many improperly enter into the throne of God by going immediately in prayer petitioning God for their needs and desires without properly giving God worship, praise, reverence, and thanksgiving.

Enter Into His Gates with Thanksgiving

You must first enter into prayer with thanksgiving. You can begin by thanking God for His great gift of our salvation through Jesus Christ. Our entire salvation is based upon God's love for us in giving Jesus Christ to die on the cross for us. I believe that this is not something we should do every Easter, or simply on Communion Sundays at our church. I believe that this is something we should do each and every day. Take time to thank Him for giving you life this day, and for giving you health, strength, and a sound and peaceful mind. Thank Him for your spouse, children, family and loved ones, and for keeping them safe. Thank Him for your shelter (your home or apartment). Thank Him for the abundance of food, water and your other provisions He has given to you.

These are things that are often taken for granted and are somewhat insignificant to many of us; but there are many people in the world, and possibly in your own city, town or even neighborhood that wish they had some of the blessings that you probably take for granted. There's a song that says, "Count your blessings and name them one by one." This simply means to take time and single out your blessings. Some Christians live their lives in depression because they always focus on what others have in comparison to what they do not have. Their eyes are always on the Jones' when in fact, they may not have as many things as the Jones', but they still nonetheless have all their needs met, and are still blessed to have much more than many others.

There's an old song I love called, *"Be Grateful."* The words to the chorus say, *"Be grateful, because there's someone else that's worse off than you. Be grateful, because there's someone else who would love to be in your shoes."* This song holds a lot of truth. As bad as we think we have it at times, there are others who would consider our bad times a tremendous blessing. When we fail to take time to thank God for His blessings, we are actually showing our ungratefulness to God.

Imagine taking your hard earned money and purchasing a nice pair of $65.00 gym shoes for your child. Now, let's say your child did not want the $65.00 gym shoes, but instead wanted a more expensive pair that cost $200.00. And, because you didn't buy your child the pair they wanted, they didn't show any appreciation, never said thank you for the ones you bought them, and instead, complained about them. Imagine how that would make you feel. You would feel that your child was ungrateful. That's how God sees us when we fail to give Him thanksgiving for our blessings. Again, we may not have all the things that we want, but God has blessed us with many things, and we should take time out and thank Him for the things in which He has blessed us. So as you enter into prayer, enter into His gates with thanksgiving by taking time and naming your blessings and giving thanksgiving to God for them.

...And into His Courts with Praise...

There are many forms of praise. We can give God praise by dancing before Him. We can give God praise by pleasing Him in living righteous and godly before Him. There are other ways that we can give Him praise. However, in this portion of the scripture, when it says, "*...and into His courts with praise,*" it is referring to the dictionary's definition of praise. The dictionary's definition of praise is this: to commend; to give adoration; to glorify.

In this kind of praise you exalt God by telling Him how great, glorious, wonderful, mighty, powerful, awesome and sovereign He is. You also exalt and magnify Him by telling Him of His mercy, kindness and love. In this praise, you do not talk about Him, but rather to Him. An example of this kind of praise can be found in the book, "*The Weapons of Our Warfare, Volume One*" in the prayer of praise and worship. This entire prayer expresses to God some of the things mentioned above. An example of some of them are listed as follows:

"How excellent is Your name in all the earth. There is no one like You, O Lord. For You are far above all nations, kings and kingdoms. You are the God of gods, the King of kings, and the Lord of lords. You are the Alpha and Omega, the First and the Last, the Beginning and the End. Before You, O Lord, there was no other, and You shall outlive eternity itself. You are clothed with beauty, strength, honor, and majesty.

You alone do great wonders throughout all the earth. With Your wisdom, You made the heavens; and with the power of Your Word, You stretched out the earth above

the waters. You gave us the sun to rule by day, and the moon and stars to rule by night. You are far above all principalities, mights, and dominions; and Your name is far above every name that is named, not only in this world, but also in that which is to come."

These two paragraphs are from the prayer, *"A Prayer of Praise and Worship."* Everything in this prayer is taken from scripture. But in praising God, you can also use your words to praise and magnify God and His awesomeness. One day I was worshipping and praising God while walking, and looked up at the sun. All of a sudden, the awesome power, might, and authority of God seemed to come alive to me. I began to praise Him for how He spoke and said, **"Let there be light,"** and from the beginning of time until now the sun has not stopped shining.

I began to tell Him how I didn't understand how man could possibly believe that the sun, which had not stopped shining from the beginning of time and never burned out, could have possibly evolved from nothing. I began to praise Him for how He created the sun to warm the earth and cause the plants to grow. I went on for about a half an hour magnifying, praising and glorifying Him for His greatness.

There was another day I was walking and looked down at a patch of grass. And it just amazed me all of a sudden how the grass, as well as the trees could grow from dirt. I then began to magnify Him—how that only He could take a few seeds and make a forest. Just thinking about His awesome creative power and authority made me bow down in the middle of the dirt, lift my hands and begin to praise and magnify Him.

You can praise Him from scriptures that deal with praise and worship, or you can praise Him in things like the examples I used above. It doesn't matter which way you do it, as long as you give Him the praise He deserves.

* Note: In the book, *The Weapons of Our Warfare, Volume III,* there are over fifty scriptures that you can use to help you magnify, praise and exalt the Lord.

Other Forms of Praise

We are not only limited to praising God with our words, we can also praise Him with our attitude and gestures. This form of praise actually goes into worship. The following are a few of them and what they represent:

The Lifting of Your Hands: The lifting of the hands represents an attitude of surrender. An example of this would be if a person pulled a gun or dangerous weapon on someone. That person would lift up their hands. This is a gesture that has existed since the dawn of civilization. When a person lifts up their hands to someone who has a dangerous weapon on them, without saying a word, they are saying the following:

1. You are in a higher position than I am
2. I am helpless to you
3. You are in control
4. I humble and submit myself to your will or control

When we lift our hands unto the Lord, we are saying the same thing. Without speaking a word, we are surrendering ourselves to Him and telling the Lord the following:

1. The Lord is High, lifted up and exalted above all.

2. We are helpless to His awesome power and might.

3. He is in complete control of our hearts, minds, and lives.

4. We humbly submit ourselves to His will and complete control.

The Clapping of Your Hands: When we clap our hands for someone, it usually means one of two things: We are either applauding their presence or their performance. If clapping for the presence of someone, it usually means that they are a high dignitary, celebrity, or in a high position of authority. If clapping for a performer, it usually means that person has performed extremely well and we were pleased with their performance. When we clap our hands to the Lord, without saying a word, we are saying this:

1. We recognize that the presence of the Lord is here, and we are grateful and thankful to be in His presence.

2. We give Him the highest honor, glory, and adoration because He alone is worthy of our praise.

The Bowing of the Knees, or Bowing with your Head to the Ground: This position represents a sign of humility. When someone bows for someone else, the person who bows is acknowledging the hierarchy of authority, power, and position of the other person. It also represents that they are at the same time acknowledging and expressing their position of humility, submission and subservience in comparison to that person. When we bow before the Lord, without saying a word we are saying this:

1. He is the most High God

2. He is high and lifted up above all

3. He is the one with all power, authority and dominion

4. We humble and submit our hearts and lives before Him

5. We are nothing in comparison to Him

6. He is our Master and Ruler , and we are His servants

There are other positions of praise but these are just a few of the most widely used positions.

Be Thankful unto Him, and Bless His Name

When we take the time to properly enter into the presence of the Lord with praise, worship, adoration, exaltation and thanksgiving, we go beyond the outer courts, to the inner courts, and finally into the holy of holies. Once we have entered into the holy of holies—into the very presence of God, we can then continue on talking to God and presenting our petitions to Him. But now, He is open and receptive to hear whatever we have to tell or ask Him.

It's like when a husband and wife come together intimately. If a man does not take the time to properly (intimately) minister to his wife, she will be somewhat reserved and unprepared to receive him. However, when the husband takes the time to properly (intimately) minister to his wife, she becomes stimulated, excited, open and receptive to receive him. In a sense, the husband has to get the wife in the mood to receive him.

It's somewhat the same way with the Lord. Before you begin petitioning the Lord for what you want or need, you have to get the Lord in the mood. When you take the time to properly minister to the Lord with praise, worship, adoration and thanksgiving, you get Him in the mood, and He becomes open to whatever you have to tell or ask Him.

———————— Chapter 4 ————————

Thy Kingdom Come

W hen Jesus said, *"thy kingdom come,"* many people think that He was instructing us to pray that the Lord would soon come and rapture up His church. But this is not what this passage is referring to at all. It was rather, an acknowledgement and understanding of the power and authority which God has given to us.

> *But if I cast out devils by the Spirit of God, then* <u>*the kingdom of God is come unto you.*</u>
> *Matthew 12:28*

Prior to this passage, the Pharisees had attributed Jesus' power to cast out devils to Beelzebub, the prince of devils. They were not denying the fact that Jesus had the power to cast out devils, because they had seen Him cast them out. However, they credited Satan as being the source of His power. Jesus responded to this accusation by saying that if He had cast out devils by the power of Satan, then Satan's kingdom would be divided by fighting against itself. He then went on to refute their accusation with the above passage, saying that if He had instead cast them out by the Spirit of God, then the power of the Kingdom of God was now available to them. Jesus was not referring to the Kingdom of God coming as when He raptures the church; He was letting the Pharisees know that the same power, dominion, and authority that He used to cast out devils was now available to man.

> *And these signs shall follow them that believe; In my name shall they cast out devils; they shall speak with new tongues...*
>
> **Mark 16:17**

Let's first clarify what Jesus meant when He said, *"And these signs shall follow them that believe."* A believer is a person who has accepted Jesus Christ into their heart and experienced the (spiritual) new birth. In Romans 10:9 it reads: *That if thou shalt confess with thy mouth the Lord Jesus, and shalt <u>believe in thine heart</u> that God hath raised him from the dead, thou shalt be saved.* Many take this passage to say that all you have to do is to believe in Jesus Christ and then you shall be saved. That's not what this passage is saying. This word "believe" comes from the Greek word *"Pistos,"* which means to receive inwardly. It's not enough to believe in Christ with your natural mind, you have to receive Him intimately into your heart. In James 2:19 it tells us that the devils believe and tremble. So this word "believe" goes beyond simply having an acknowledgement in your head; it goes deeper into having an intimate experience in your heart with the Lord.

In order for a woman to get pregnant, her egg must mix with the seed of a man. When they mix together, they begin the embryonic stage of new life. Likewise, when a sinner hears the Word of God preached, faith comes alive in their heart to receive. They must then open up their heart to receive Christ. Once they do, their faith combines with the Word of God they have heard, and the new birth experience takes place in their life. This is why the new birth experience is called being born again—because it is a spiritual birthing experience. So, when Jesus said, *"And these signs shall follow them that believe,"* He was referring to those who have received Christ intimately into their hearts and have gone through the new birth experience.

Jesus was saying that the believer (every believer) has the power to cast out devils and walk in the power of the miraculous. Many denominations and religions teach that only the pastor, priest or high spiritual leaders of the church possess this ability. I was listening to a particular Christian broadcast on the radio and heard a Christian leader say that layman Christians do not possess the power to cast out devils. He went on to say that this is something that should be left up to trained spiritual leaders. I was appalled that this spiritual leader was teaching this incorrect doctrine.

It's not attending a seminary, being assigned to a position or title in the church, or receiving a diploma, license, or ordination papers that give you the power and authority to cast out devils and walk in the miraculous. It's having the anointing of God that is available to every born-again believer.

> *And he said unto them, Verily I say unto you, that there be some of them that stand here, which shall not taste of death, till they have seen the kingdom of God come with power.*
>
> *Mark 9:1*

Jesus was telling them that some of them would not die before seeing the manifestation of the Kingdom of God (the power of God) being available to and coming upon man.

> *And heal the sick that are therein, and say unto them, <u>the kingdom of God is come</u> nigh unto you.*
>   *Luke 10:9*

In this passage Jesus was giving instructions to His disciples. He told them to go about healing the sick and telling them (all the people) that the Kingdom of God was nigh unto them. In other words, God was just about ready to bestow the same power upon them that Jesus had to heal the sick and walk in the miraculous. The reason why He said that it was near to them was because, first, Jesus had to be crucified upon the cross and ascend to the Father. This was near (referring to time) actually taking place. Once Christ had been crucified, He ascended to the Father, and God sent the Holy Spirit to us to not only dwell upon us, but to also dwell within us. It's the power of God through the Holy Spirit that enables us to walk in the miraculous.

> *But ye shall receive power, after that the Holy Ghost is come upon you: and ye shall be witnesses unto me both in Jerusalem, and in all Judaea, and in Samaria, and unto the uttermost part of the earth.*
>   *Acts 1:8*

"Thy Kingdom Come" represents the *"Power"* the above passage is talking about. Jesus went on to say in this passage that we would become His witnesses. This word "witness" is actually the word "representative." In a city or

municipality the police force represents that city or municipality. When the police go on duty, they are authorized by
the city to use deadly force. This means that they can le-
gally use their weapons (if necessary) or whatever means
available to them to stop or apprehend those who disobey
the law.

In the same manner, God has anointed us as His repre-
sentatives (*witnesses*) to uphold the law of His Word. John
10:10 describes Satan as the thief that comes to steal, kill
and destroy. God has given us the power and authority to
use deadly force against Satan and his demonic spirits and
cohorts. You have been spiritually deputized by God to
represent Him in binding the devil, pulling down strongholds, and casting them out.

> **Neither shall they say, Lo here! or, lo there! for,
> behold, <u>the kingdom of God is within you</u>.**
> *Luke 17:21*

This passage validates the point we made earlier about
the power of God dwelling within us. Jesus is describing to
them a time soon to come (after His death, burial and res-
urrection) when the power of God would be available to all
believers. That time came when Christ rose from the dead
and the power of the Holy Ghost was poured upon the
church. It is now available to you. Casting out devils is
available for you. Laying hands upon the sick to receive
healing is available to you. Walking in the miraculous
power of God is available to you! So when Jesus said, "***thy
kingdom come***," it was to remind us of the authority of
God through Christ that is available to us.

In most of the prayers in our prayer handbook series,
you will find a passage that says something similar to this:

"Now Father, I thank You for the authority that you have given us in Christ Jesus; and with that authority, I bind every demonic spirit...."

"Thy kingdom come" represents an acknowledgement of the power and authority you now have as a child of God. It also represents an acknowledgement that this power and authority does not come by your might, wisdom, or strength, but rather, by God through Jesus Christ.

The devil would have you to be ignorant. He doesn't want you to know that you can bind him and put him in his place. The reason he wants to keep you ignorant to this fact is that you can only walk in this power and authority if you first of all know you have it, and secondly, when you exercise your authority.

There's a saying that goes, "what you don't know won't hurt you." This couldn't be the farthest thing from the truth regarding prayer and spiritual warfare. In prayer and spiritual warfare, not knowing your position of power and authority in Christ can not only hurt you, but can destroy you spiritually. In Hosea 4:6, God said, *"my people are destroyed because of a lack of knowledge."* It's Satan that is doing the destroying. He is destroying lives, marriages, homes and many other facets of the lives of God's people simply because we don't know that the kingdom of God (power and authority of God) has already come and is now available to us.

Don't be a victim of Satan's destruction. Learn about your place and position you have in Christ, and begin to exercise your authority to speak the Word of God and put Satan where he belongs in your life (under your feet). This is why it is important that you constantly rehearse scriptures that fill your heart with faith of who you are in Christ.

When Jesus said, *"thy kingdom come,"* the principle of prayer He was teaching us is that we have to remind ourselves of, and rehearse (through the Word of God) our position of authority. It is important that you find scriptures that build up your faith and confidence that you are not only a child of God, but that you are also a king who has been commissioned and anointed to rule, reign, and dominate, rather than having Satan to rule, reign and dominate you.

* Note: In the book, *"The Weapons of our Warfare, Volume III,"* there is a confession of authority that I believe that every born again believer should have. It is over 6 pages long, and has over 40 scriptures that will build your heart up in faith and power, and prepare you to not only talk like a king, but to also walk in your kingship authority and power through Christ Jesus. I encourage every Christian to rehearse this confession, or at least something similar to it at least once or twice a week.

The following are a few other additional scriptures that will help you to understand the Kingdom power that God has made available to you.

> *And hath made us kings and priests unto God and His Father; to Him be glory and dominion for ever and ever. Amen.*
>
> ***Revelation 1:6***

The job of a king is to rule and reign. Just as Adam had the initial job of ruling over the earth, God has called us as kings to also rule and reign over the earth. You are a king. Learn your position of authority you have in Christ and begin to walk in your kingship authority.

Where the word of a king is, there is power...
                                    Ecclesiastes 8:4

A king does not rule by his sheer might and strength. A king rules with the power and authority of his word. He gives commands, orders, and decrees. Likewise, we are to also rule like a king with our words. However, we are not to use our words, but rather, the Word of the living God.

> ***Thou shalt also decree a thing, and it shall be established unto thee: and the light shall shine upon thy ways.***
>
> > ***Job 22:28***

In ancient days, when the king made an official decree, it could not be revoked. As kings, God has given us the authority to decree and declare His Word. And as we do so, just as the word of a king had to come to pass, the Word of God that we speak will also come to pass.

We must understand that we are not merely helpless imbeciles against the onslaught of Satan, but rather, a predominant force (through Christ) against him. Our position in Spiritual Warfare is not one that sits on the side at the mercy of Satan, but one of power, dominion, and authority over him.

> ***And I will give unto thee the keys of the kingdom of heaven: and whatsoever thou shalt bind on earth shall be bound in heaven: and whatsoever thou shalt loose on earth shall be loosed in heaven.***
>
> > ***Matthew 16:19***

Many incorrectly spend all their time begging God to

deliver them. But as kings, God has given us the keys to the kingdom, which represent His power and authority. Therefore, we don't have to sit back and be victimized by the devil. God is waiting on us to take our proper position of authority. Jesus said, whatever we bind on earth shall be bound in the heavens, and whatever we loose on earth shall be loosed in the heavens. What this is saying is that whatever we bind with our natural, physical words will be bound in the spiritual realm. And whatever we loose with our natural words will be loosed in the spiritual realm. In other words, as we know, Satan is the motivator and instigator of the attacks against us. But as kings, when we bind him, God causes the authority of our natural words to bind Satan in the spiritual realm. And as we loose him with our natural words, our authority forces Satan to loose his hold from our lives in the spiritual realm. And once we effectively deal with Satan and his demonic spirits in the spiritual realm, our situations and circumstances in the natural realm will soon change.

For example, if there is trouble or turmoil in your marriage, you need to understand that Satan is the one who is instigating the trouble. As you bind him, he is spiritually bound, tied up, and can no longer instigate further trouble against your marriage. When you command him to loose his hold from your marriage, he has no choice but to follow your decree and command and take his hands off further influence upon your marriage. And as you bind and loose him in the spiritual realm from your marriage, things in the natural realm regarding your marriage will soon change.

And God said, Let us make man in our image, after our likeness: <u>and let them have dominion...</u>
Genesis 1:26

This was the original plan of God for man. It was to rule, dictate, and dominate. When Adam sinned, man lost his kingship authority and position. But when Jesus died on the cross, He re-established man (those who are born again) to his original position of dominion and authority. It was never intended by God for Satan to rule, dictate, and dominate your life. Instead, it was intended that you dictate and dominate him and his demonic spirits. Neither was it ever intended by God for your situations and circumstances to rule, dictate and dominate your life; it was intended for you to dominate them instead.

Your position of dominion as a born-again believer is to dominate your health (walk in good health), dominate your finances (walk in prosperity and the blessings of God), and every aspect of your life. *"Thy Kingdom Come"* represents this kingship position of ruling and dominating. It is imperative that you begin to realize that the Kingdom of God has come unto you, and that His power and authority is now available to you to walk in your (intended) position of dominion and authority. Once you realize this and begin to exercise and walk in your position of authority and dominion, the things in your life will change. Instead of them dictating and dominating your life, you will begin to dictate and dominate them instead.

So once again, *"thy kingdom come"* represents the acknowledgement and attitude that God has given us His power and authority to represent Him in the earth realm. We are to utilize His power to rule and reign over demons and demonic spirits, and destroy the works of Satan in our lives and in the lives of others, as well as dominate the situations and circumstances in our lives.

* Note: To find more about your authority in Christ, see our book entitled, *"Praying in Your Divine Authority."*

Chapter 5

Thy Will Be Done

We all know that God is omnipotent, all mighty and all-powerful. We also know that God can do whatever He desires to do. But the question is this: Is God's will automatically done in the earth? The answer to this question may surprise many, but the answer is "no." To explain this we need to go back to the story of Adam again. When God put Adam on the earth, He set him over the earth. When Adam sinned and disobeyed God, he gave up his position of authority over the earth. Satan then took Adam's place. In 2 Cor. 4:4, the Bible calls Satan the god of this world. He is the god of this world in principal, not power or authority. However, even though he is the god of this world, we (the children of God) inhabit this earth, and we (as inhabitants of the earth) have the right to invite the will of God into the earth.

For I know the thoughts that I think toward you,
saith the LORD, thoughts of peace, and not of
evil, to give you an expected end.

Jeremiah 29:11

This passage shows us God's desire to bless us with peace and see us blessed and prosperous. But even though it is God's desire for us to be blessed, we must still invite His will in our lives if we want to experience His blessings.

And be not conformed to this world: but be ye
transformed by the renewing of your mind, that
ye may prove what is that good, and acceptable,
and perfect, will of God.

Romans 12:2

The earth, as well as those who are in the earth is constantly going through a type of metamorphosis. Spiritually speaking, there is a spiritual metamorphosis continually going on also. This metamorphosis is a change into the pattern, style and likeness of the world. If a person does not do anything to resist this change, they will eventually evolve into the likeness and pattern of the world — meaning, they will begin to talk, act and live like a non-Christian. However, if they begin a life of prayer and confession in the Word of God, instead of becoming conformed to the pattern and likeness of the world, they will become transformed into the life and image of Christ instead.

Having said all this, now let's go back to the matter of the will of God in the earth. Just as you must do something to counteract the conformity of the world in your life, you must likewise do something to counteract Satan's will in your life.

The thief cometh not, but for to steal, and to kill, and to destroy: I am come that they might have life, and that they might have it more abundantly.
John 10:10

There are primarily two influential sources in our lives. Our lives will either be influenced and changed for the negative by Satan and his will to bring killing, stealing and destruction to the situations and circumstances of our lives, or it will be influenced by the will of God. Satan's will is to destroy our peace, marriage, family, job, finances, children, and every aspect of our lives. And, if we don't do anything to counteract his rampage of destruction, that's exactly what we will experience.

On the other hand, we have the will of God. God's desire and will for our lives is to not only give us the eternal life of heaven, but to also give us the abundant life of His blessings, prosperity, good health, protection and favor here on earth. We are God's children, but although He desires to bless us, He cannot do it unless we invite His will in our lives.

As you enter into prayer each day, you must verbally invite God's will to come in your life. You are to do this each and every day that you pray. Again, remember, God cannot, and will not force His will upon your life. You are the one who must give Him an invitation to come into your life. It's the same when a person gives their life to the Lord. Although the Lord has made salvation available to all who will accept Him, He will not force His free gift of salvation upon us. He will only bring salvation to those who open up their lives and invite Him in. Likewise, He will only bring His will upon those who also invite His will into their lives.

Each day you are to invite God's will to be done in your life, marriage, business, and other key areas of your life. At the same time, you are to pray and shut the door and bind Satan's will of killing, stealing, and destruction from your life. This portion of your prayer may sound something like this:

"Father, I invite You to send Your angels to carry out your will to be done in the earth as Your will is done in heaven. Father, I invite your will to be done in my life, and every aspect of my life this day. I ask for Your will to not only be done in my life, but also in the lives of my children, in my marriage, my spouse's life, and in the lives of my family. I pray for Your will to be done in our lives to keep us in good health. I pray for Your will to be done in our finances and upon our jobs to bring blessings, prosperity and promotions. May Your will be done in each and every area and aspect of our lives in the name of Jesus Christ."

As we said earlier, there are only two sources in the world. You have the source or will of God, and you have the source or will of the devil. Only one of them will be carried out and manifested in your life. It simply depends on which one you choose to invite into your life. You can either go into prayer each day and invite the will of God in your life—which is to give you His blessings, prosperity, protection, and favor, or you can do nothing, and thereby invite the will of Satan into your life—which is to bring killing, stealing and destruction to your situations and circumstances. The choice is yours.

Chapter 6

Give us this Day, Our Daily Bread

Whean Jesus said, *"give us this day our daily bread,"* it represents two things: First, it represents the frequency of praying every day. Secondly, the bread represents things that are essential in prayer. Physically, bread is essential for us to live. Likewise, there are things in life that are also essential for us and should be prioritized in prayer. In this passage, Jesus is teaching us that these things should be prayed about each and every day. These essentials of our daily bread, or rather, "daily needs" represent things such as our protection, provisions, direction, and health.

As we pray each day, we are to ask God to watch over us and assign His angels to protect us from hurt, harm, and danger. We should pray that He would continually provide for us things we need such as food, water, clothing, and shelter. We should pray that He would direct us by His Spirit and lead and guide us through our day in the decisions and choices we need to make. We should pray that He would keep us in good health—continually healed by the stripes of Jesus Christ. And along with these requests, we should pray for any other thing we feel is essential to us in life.

Spiritual Essentials

Our "daily bread" not only consists of us praying for our natural needs, it also consists of us praying for our spiritual needs. Spiritual needs are areas in our lives that either we know we are weak in and need help, or areas in which the Holy Spirit has shown us that we need to pray for more strength or faith. This should include any area in your life in which Satan either has a stronghold now, or has had one in the recent past. Whether the problem is (or was) drugs, alcohol, lust, lying, or any other type of stronghold, it should be prayed about every day.

Any time a person has been victimized by Satan and it has led to them having a stronghold, that stronghold becomes the equivalence of having a wound. If a person becomes hospitalized or is under care for some type of wound, it is imperative that their dressing be changed every day. If the dressing is not changed every day, infection could easily set in, and the problem could escalate to widespread infection or even gangrene.

Every time you pray over a problem, it's the equivalence of changing the dressing and cleaning the wound. Many Christians allow Satan to continue to dominate them or keep them in spiritual bondage because they do not adhere to this principle.

Spiritual Vacations

Many Christians take what I call "Spiritual Vacations." A spiritual vacation is when you pray like you should one day, but you take the next day or even several days off from your daily prayer and devotion. Let's say that Sunday morning before church you had a good prayer and touched the throne of God. But because of your busy schedule and other distractions, you did not pray Monday or Tuesday. This would be a spiritual vacation. By the time you get back in the routine of prayer on Wednesday (because of your spiritual vacation), spiritual infection could have set in. Spiritual infection works like a natural infection. It's when we give Satan a place to not only keep us in bondage in the area in which we may have been struggling, but to allow him to also strengthen his hold on that area and even get a hold on other areas in our lives.

One of the biggest tricks of Satan is to try to consume your time and make you feel that you don't have time to pray. While you are on your spiritual vacation, Satan and his demon spirits are not on vacation, but diligently and fervently working against you. By the time you pick up on prayer a few days later, they have already been busy working, trying to bring destruction to your life. Here is the deception: Many people feel that just because they are not having any problems at the current time that things are all right; but that's the deception of Satan. The work that he does against us in the spiritual realm does not take manifestation until later. In other words, the trials you may be experiencing this week or this month may be a result of the spiritual vacation you took last week or last month. Jesus understood this principle. This is why He instructed us to pray for our daily bread every day.

An Old Testament Example of Our Daily Bread

An Old Testament example of us praying for our daily bread can be found in Exodus Chapters 15 and 16. In this passage, God had delivered the children of Israel out of Egypt and brought them across the Red Sea on dry land. Shortly afterwards, they began to murmur and complain about not having food, so God sent them Manna (bread) from heaven.

God literally rained Manna from heaven each day. God had given specific instructions for Moses to give the people regarding the Manna. When the Manna fell, they were only to get enough for each member of the household. They were also only to get enough manna for the current day.

The only exception was for the Sabbath day. Because of the Old Testament's strict rules regarding any type of work or labor on the Sabbath day, they could get twice as much on the sixth day to prepare their portion for the Sabbath day.

Knowing human nature, even if you have never read this account before, you already know what happened. As expected, there were many that ignored God's instructions to Moses and the people of Israel, and attempted to stock-pile a little extra for the next day. Some may have tried to store extra for the next day because they wanted twice as much to eat. Some may have done it because of fear that the Manna would cease and not fall. Others simply may have been trying to get enough in order to save the work and effort of having to get and prepare the Manna the next day. Whatever the reason, it was against God's directions and His Word for them to do it. Those who disobeyed God found that when they awakened the next morning, the extra Manna they tried to save had turned to worms and began to stink profusely. They quickly learned that God meant what He said about only getting enough for that day.

This daily supply of Manna, and God's instructions concerning it is a natural image of several spiritual principles concerning "Our Daily Bread." It first of all represents the frequency of prayer. Once again, God sent the Manna every day (except the Sabbath day).

Some Christians think or feel that because they may have had a good prayer or long prayer one day, that it gives them the luxury or affordability to be able to skip a day or so of prayer (spiritual vacation). In a sense, they feel that they have stockpiled enough intimacy with God or prayer power against the enemy that they can afford to skip a day of prayer. But just as the Manna stank when it was left over the next day, our left over prayers stink before God the same way.

When I say "left over prayers," I am referring to the mentality of some that their prayer for one day is good enough to last or suffice for the next day. Just as God did not want the children of Israel to attempt to save extra Manna for the next day, but rather get a fresh daily supply each day, Jesus was also instructing us to make sure that we come before God in prayer each day to get a fresh supply of His presence, power, and anointing. Skipping a day of prayer has the same significance as the children of Israel attempting to stockpile enough Manna for the next day. Once again, it stinks before God and is no good.

Incidentally, some people feel that because they are going to church Sunday morning that they do not have to pray on Sunday. Some would even look at the account we just mentioned about the Children of Israel and conclude that since they did not have to get Manna on the Sabbath day, that we shouldn't have to pray on the Sabbath day. This belief is totally incorrect. Let me insert this about the Sabbath day. The Sabbath day was not made for God; it was made for man. God made the human body. He understands what it needs. He also understands that it needs rest. God created the Sabbath day as a day for man to have rest. Although we may not adhere to the strict practical Old Testament law of not doing any work or physical labor on the Sabbath day, we should still have a Sabbath day, or at least a day where we get some rest.

When you work from sun up to sun down, you not only wear yourself down physically, but also mentally and even spiritually. When your spirit-man becomes weak, the devil is able to sneak into your life. The Sabbath day was instituted by God to not only allow rest for the physical body, but to also allow the spiritual body time to be restored and renewed. Therefore, Sunday is not a day that we should take off from prayer simply because we are going to church. Even if you are going to pray at church, you still need your personal, intimate time with God.

Don't Give Your Flesh An Inch

The next parallel I would like to make with this passage in Exodus is that as Christians, we cannot afford to take a day off from prayer. Even if you have never heard the story of what happened to the Children of Israel, at a certain point, you can guess what happened to them as a result of their disobedience. If we can understand this type of human greed, then we can also understand another principle of human nature. Have you ever heard the saying, "Give them an inch, and they will take a mile?" In other words, if you give some people just a little space, they will want to take a lot. Well, that's how our flesh is regarding prayer.

You must understand that you are made up of spirit, soul, and body. Jesus said in Matthew 26:41, "*...the spirit indeed is willing, but the flesh is weak.*" Your spirit man wants to pray and seek the face of God, but your flesh and soul get nothing out of prayer. If you allow yourself to skip a day of prayer, it becomes harder to pray the next day. Once you skip a day of prayer, your soul will begin to rationalize the reason for not praying the next day. It may be because you're tired one day. The next reason may be because you have so many things to do. The next day you may just accept any reason from the devil for not praying, until finally, you get comfortable not praying at all, and the devil just walks right in your life.

Your Soul Does Not Want to Pray

Have you ever struggled to pray in the morning? I am not talking about the struggle we sometimes have trying to break through to that secret, intimate place with God; nor am I talking about struggling to get time to spend with God. I'm talking about the struggle just to open your mouth and pray. I believe that every Christian experiences this struggle from time to time.

If you have ever felt like this before, you are not alone. I have people call me all the time expressing this difficulty in prayer. There are days even in my own life that my soul would rather go outside and cut the grass (something I truly dread doing) than pray. If you have had this difficulty before, the following scripture describes what you were experiencing.

*For the flesh lusteth [war] against the Spirit, and
the Spirit [also war] against the flesh: and these
are contrary the one to the other: so that ye cannot do the things that ye would.*

Galatians 5:17

Your flesh fights against your spirit. Again, Jesus said in
Matthew 26:41, *"... the spirit indeed is willing, but the flesh
is weak."* Your spirit wants to pray and seek the face of
God. However, your soul does not want to pray. It gets
nothing out of prayer, and will fight you every step of the
way to keep you from praying. This is why you must be
disciplined to pray. It is Satan using your soul to fight
against your spirit. The more you discipline your soul to
pray and not allow it the chance to take "Spiritual Vacations," the easier the struggle will become. But, when you
skip a day or so of prayer, you are un-disciplining your
soul and therefore allowing it the chance to get out of control (like a spoiled child) and attempt to keep you from
prayer.

Again, you must remember that your soul is like a child.
You have to make your children do things that are good
for them even when they don't like doing them. If you do
not stay on them to do the things they should do daily
(such as take a bath or brush their teeth), and you allow
them to stop, it will become harder to get them back in the
habit of doing them again. It's the same way with our soul
regarding prayer. If you take a day off from prayer one
day, it may lead to several days. And, after the soul gets
comfortable not praying, it becomes a struggle getting it
back in the daily discipline of prayer.

Just about every one knows that we are in a spiritual
warfare. When you are in war, there are no Sundays off, no
vacations, and no time to let your guard down. If an army

took this attitude in war and took days off, the opposing force would easily overtake them. It's the same thing in our spiritual warfare. If we take time off, we allow our opposing force (Satan) to advance on us. It truly takes discipline, diligence and determination to come before God daily in prayer. The devil will constantly send distractions against you to attempt to keep you from praying. Satan will do everything he can to stop you from praying. He will use your children, spouse, family members, friends, and anyone or anything he can to hinder you from getting your daily bread. Don't let the devil seduce you into taking a day off from prayer; become disciplined in prayer to come before the Lord "daily."

Ye Have Not Because Ye Ask Not

Some people wonder why they have to ask God for what they need when He already knows what they need. God does know what we need, but He has also established rules and guidelines by which we are to follow in order get what we need from Him — by asking.

> *Ye have not, because ye ask not. Ye ask, and receive not, because ye ask amiss...* — James 4:2-3

In this passage James gives two reasons why we lack many of our needs and desires. One of the reasons James explains why we do not get our needs and desires met is because we ask amiss — the wrong way. The other reason is because we simply don't ask. God requires us to ask Him for whatever we need. He wants us to know that all of our provisions and blessings come from Him. But just as He wants us to know this, He also wants us to know that they are there for the asking. God has established prayer as the vehicle in which we are to use to talk to Him. He is our Father, and He is willing to give us whatever we need as long as we ask for it.

All throughout the New Testament you find that before Jesus healed someone, He would often ask them, *"what do you need for me to do for you?"* To ask someone a question like this who was blind, crippled, lame or demon possessed would seem somewhat rhetorical, or even insensitive, seeming that Jesus should obviously already know what they needed. But He asked them for a particular purpose. He needed them to verbally ask for what they needed.

When the scripture says that we *"ask not,"* I believe that there is a way in which you can ask, and yet still not ask. I know that this may sound somewhat confusing, but let me explain. Let's say a person has a job, but that employee is the kind of worker that is an employer's nightmare. They come to work late all the time; they don't want to do their job; they take too long for lunch; they leave early; and they always call in sick. This person may say, "I want and need my job;" but although they are saying they want and need their job, their actions are showing otherwise.

There's a cliché that says, *"actions speak louder than words."* In other words, you can say something with your mouth, but your actions can show otherwise. This employee is saying they want their job, but their actions are speaking louder and saying they "do not" want to keep their job. And, with these kinds of actions (work ethics) they would certainly lose their job.

When the scripture says that we have not because we ask not, I believe that it is also saying that although we periodically come to God in prayer and ask for what we need, that we are sometimes so halfhearted in our prayer (in being disciplined to pray each day and spend quality time with God in prayer), that we become like the employee who says that he wants to keep his job, but his actions say that he doesn't. I believe that with God, when we are halfhearted in our requests, petitions and time with Him in prayer, that although we are (periodically) saying out of our mouth that we need the Lord to bless us, with our lethargic actions of prayer, it's like we are not asking at all.

Your Daily Anointing

But my horn shalt thou exalt like the horn of an unicorn: I shall be anointed with fresh oil.
Psalms 92:10

The anointing of God represents His presence upon us. We cannot do anything for God without His anointing. Without His anointing, we are just mortal man. Samson had superhuman strength, but his strength represented the anointing. When God's anointing (presence) is upon us, we become (like Samson) superhuman beings.

Samson allowing Delilah to seduce him into telling her his secret and cutting his hair, represents us allowing the devil to cut off our anointing. With the anointing of God upon Samson, he could slay wild beasts with his bare hands, and defeat an entire army by himself. However, after his hair was cut, the Bible says that he arose thinking that he had the strength to do what he had done before, but did not know that the Lord's strength (anointing) had departed from him, and he became a normal man.

When we get in the presence of God and properly pray each day, in the spiritual realm, we become like Samson.

Samson's call was to destroy the Philistines. Spiritually, the Philistines represent demons and demonic spirits. God has called you to be a demon and devil slayer. But in order for you to walk in this awesome power of God, you must come daily in the presence of God and get a fresh portion of His anointing. When you spend quality time with God in prayer, the glory and anointing of the Lord will come upon you (like Samson), and you will be able to put the devil where he belongs in your life, which is under your feet.

The above passage says, *"We shall be anointed with fresh oil."* When we come before God (daily) in prayer, that's exactly what happens. We get anointed with the freshness of His presence. It is imperative that we come before Him each day to get our daily dose of His presence upon us. If we are not diligent and disciplined to pray each day, the anointing will lift from us, and we will become ineffective for the Kingdom of God, and ineffective against the kingdom of darkness.

It's like engine oil in a car. The engine oil lubricates the parts of the engine and keeps them from rubbing against each other and wearing out. If the engine oil is not changed in the proper amount of time, it will lose its viscosity or ability to effectively lubricate the engine parts. Once the oil loses its viscosity, even though it is still considered oil, it becomes ineffective in lubricating the parts, and they quickly and easily wear out. Likewise, if we fail to come before God daily in prayer, we will also lose our anointing and effectiveness against the devil and demonic spirits (the spiritual Philistines), and the enemy can then overcome us.

Faith In The Word

So then faith cometh by hearing, and hearing by the Word of God.

Romans 10:17

It is important to us as Christians to also obtain a daily supply of the Word of God in order to stay in faith. Some people think that faith is simply a matter of believing hard enough. Faith does not come because you believe hard enough; it comes from the Word of God. Reading, studying, and confessing the Word of God does the same thing to your faith and your spiritual-man as lifting weights and exercise does for the body. If you were to find someone who had a fit, muscular body and ask them how they became so physically fit and muscular, they would not tell you that they simply wanted it bad enough; they would tell you that they had to discipline themselves to diligently exercise and lift weights. Likewise, faith does not come because we believe; it comes when we exercise ourselves in the Word of God.

The above passage says that faith comes by *"hearing and hearing"* (continually hearing the Word of God). This phrase "hearing and hearing" refers to a continual process. Faith does not come because you heard the Word of God in the past; it comes as a result of continually hearing the Word. I have heard many people say that they have read the Bible before and know what the Bible says; therefore, they do not feel that they need to continually read the Bible. If you were attempting to simply read the Bible for knowledge and information, that may hold to be true. But you do not read the Bible solely for knowledge and information; you also read it to stay strong in the Lord and in your faith in Christ. Each time you read the Word of God, it builds up your faith in God. Whatever you read a month ago gave you the faith for that particular time. However, if you need faith for something "now" in a particular area, you would need to currently read the Word of God to give you faith for what you are going through "now."

Taking the Medicine of the Word

Now faith is the substance of things hoped for, the evidence of things not seen.

Hebrews 11:1

The above passage helps us to establish the point we were making above. Notice, it says, "***Now Faith.***" Again, faith must be "now" or rather, "current." It's like taking medicine. Let's say that a person took a dose of penicillin for an infection they had 6 months ago. That dose of penicillin may have been good for the infection they had 6 months ago, but if they had another infection this month, the penicillin they took 6 months ago will not do anything for their current infection. They would need to get another dose of penicillin for their current infection.

Now, let's use this same example concerning a person's healing. Let's say in January someone named John became sick. Let's also say that John got into the Word of God and began to pray and confess the Word of God concerning his sickness, and received his healing. Let's also say that John became sick again in July. If this happened, John could not rely on the fact that he got into the Word in January concerning his healing. He would have to go back and pray again, read the same scriptures, and make the same confessions he made in January in order to receive his healing in

July. Again, when it says "now faith," it is saying that you must always have a current, continuing supply of faith that comes from the continual digestion of reading and studying the Word of God.

The Nourishment of the Word

Just as food and water go together, prayer and reading and confessing the Word also go together. When I say "the nourishment of the Word," I'm referring to the nourishment we get from reading, studying and confessing the Word of the Lord. When we eat natural food, it is first swallowed and travels to the stomach where it mixes with our digestive juices that help break down the food. It then enters the small intestines where it is broken down even further.

Beginning in the small intestines and continuing in the large intestines, the body then begins to absorb nutrients, vitamins and other essentials from the broken down food. It is the vitamins and nutrients that our bodies absorb from the food that gives us strength and energy. If you do not get enough nutrients and vitamins in your body, you will lose energy, become weak, and your body may become susceptible to infection and disease. Likewise in the spiritual realm, when you read, study and meditate on the Word of God, your spirit does the same thing. Your spirit also absorbs the spiritual vitamins and nutrients from the Word of God (the spiritual bread of Life).

> *Finally, my brethren, be strong in the Lord, and in the power of His might.*
>
> *Ephesians 6:10*

In this passage God encourages us to "be strong." In order for God to tell us to "be strong," we must have the ability to get strength and become strong. In the natural we know of ways to gain strength. We do it through proper eating and exercise. It's the same way in the spiritual realm. The more we (properly) eat of God's Word, the stronger our spirit will become. And, the more we exercise our faith by confessing and believing in the Word, the more strength we will gain.

Again, when we do not consume enough natural food, our body will not be able to absorb the vitamins and nutrients it needs, and can therefore become malnourished, weak and susceptible to sickness and disease. And, when we do not (daily) consume our spiritual food (the Word of God), our spirit-man can also become weak and susceptible to the deceptions, tricks and temptations of the devil. So when Jesus said, "give us this day our daily bread," He was also saying to pray that the Father would give you your daily supply of spiritual strength, energy and revelation from His Word.

A False Balance

A false balance is abomination to the LORD: but a just weight is his delight.

Proverbs 11:1

A false balance before the Lord is when you allow your time, heart, and mind to become consumed with the desires and entertainments of the world, while at the same time you do not have the same heart, mind and passion for the things of God. Please don't misunderstand me. God understands that we must work in order to live and maintain ourselves in the world. Some jobs require long hours. God understands this. He is not saying that we should not work, or even work hard and long hours if necessary. But at the same time, you cannot forget the Lord in the process and pursuit of earning the money.

A *"just weight"* before the Lord means that no matter how hard you must work, how long the hours, or how emotionally or physically draining your work may be, make sure that you also make time for the spiritual things of God in your life as well. You must make time for prayer in the morning. You must make time to read and study the Word of God. And, you must make time for church.

I have a simple personal rule for my life that helps to keep me balanced with spending time before the Lord. It is this: I do not allow myself the luxury of watching television in the evening unless I have taken the time to "properly" pray and spend time in the Word of God. I emphasize "properly pray" because it must be a balance.

Some people can barely spend 15 minutes in devotion with the Lord, but yet they can come home from work in the evening and spend two to three hours watching television. A just weight or proper balance does not mean that you cannot work long hours if necessary; nor does it mean that you cannot have any fun or entertainment. It simply means that you must make a priority to also spend time with the Lord. Again, God understands that you must work. But somewhere in your long hours of work, you must press your way to spend time with God. And, if you don't have time for God (which you should make some time for Him no matter how much work you may do), then you definitely shouldn't have time for entertainment either.

You need to ask yourself, "Am I out of balance?" If you spend all of your time working and do not make any time for the Lord, then you are out of balance. If you have little or no time for God in your day, but yet can spend time watching television as well as enjoy other entertainment, you are out of balance. Begin to balance the scales in your life by changing your priorities and make time for the Lord.

How Long Should We Pray

People often ask me this question: "What is the proper amount of time we should spend in prayer and devotion with God?" In *Matthew 26:40* Jesus asked His disciples, *"Could you not watch [pray] with me [at least] one hour?"* I believe that an hour of devotion time is the least amount of time we should spend with the Lord each day.

Some people argue and say that the amount of time we spend with the Lord each day is not important, but to simply spend time with Him. If this were true, why then would Jesus have specified *"one hour"* as the minimum amount of time He expected the disciples to have been praying? If you cannot spend an hour in prayer and devotion in the morning, then try to at least spend an hour in your combined time of morning, noon, and evening devotion.

Studying God's Word

There are two ways of studying God's Word. One way is to study for information, and the second is for meditation. Studying for information is when you familiarize yourself with the events and stories in the Bible. For example, you may feel led one day to read the story about Samson. There may be another time that you feel led to read about Paul and His letters to the Corinthian church. You may also choose to begin reading at the beginning of a particular book and read a few chapters each day until you finish the book. There are thousands of characters and stories in the Bible for us to read. It is important for us to read and get the information (historical facts) about what happened, because it is from the information/historical facts that God gives us revelation knowledge concerning our lives.

The other way that you read or study God's Word is for meditation. Meditation is to take either one scripture or a short passage and meditate on it. I remember when I was a new Christian and I attended a church in which the pastor told everyone to read at least three to five chapters in the Bible a day. Before I went to bed each night I would attempt to read three to five chapters in obedience to my pastor. But by the time I reached the end of the last chapter, I couldn't remember anything I had read.

Not only could I not remember anything I had read, I didn't get much spiritually from what I had read either. I eventually became frustrated and wondered if my reading was doing any good. After much prayer about this problem, the Lord corrected my heart and showed me what I was doing wrong.

The first problem was attempting to read three chapters of the Bible at night. When you are exhausted, first of all, your mind will have a problem retaining large amounts of information. In addition to your mind not being able to receive and retain large amounts of information, your spirit likewise will have the same difficulty. The Lord instructed me to begin reading in the morning or on my lunch break. If I did read in the evening, it needed to be earlier in the evening, and not late at night before going to bed. During these times my mind was fresh and my spirit was open to not only hear and receive the Word of God, but to also retain it.

God instructed me to meditate upon His Word at night. Reading for meditation is different from reading for information. Reading for meditation is when you take a short passage and you simply think upon or meditate on that scripture. I began doing this each night. I would take one scripture or one short passage and lie back in my bed and meditate on that scripture or passage over and over again. I would sometimes meditate on the same scripture for several days.

After a few moments, God would begin revealing something to me about that passage of scripture. Once I began reading at night for meditation and not for information, I would get more out of one scripture or passage than I had previously received from reading five chapters.

Whether you read and study for information or for meditation, you begin reading what is called the "Logos." The Logos is the written Word of God. Once you read the Logos, God begins to reveal to you what is called the "Rhema." The Rhema is the revealed Word of God. As you read for information and meditation, God reveals revelation and application to you.

> *And He said unto them, he that hath ears to hear, let him hear. And when He was alone, they that were about him with the twelve asked of Him the parable. And He said unto them, unto you it is given to know the mystery of the kingdom of God: but unto them that are without all these things are done in parables.*
>
> **Mark 4:9-11**

In the book of Mark chapter 4, Jesus gave a parable about the sower. After He finished the parable, no one understood the meaning. They did not understand it because Jesus had simply given them the Logos (the written Word of God). The above passage shows the disciples coming to Jesus and asking Him for an understanding of the meaning of the parable. In verses 14 through 20, Jesus gave them the understanding of the parable. The understanding of this parable would be referred to as the Rhema. Without Jesus revealing the Rhema, their understanding of this parable would have been void.

This is the reason why people who are not Christians do not understand the Bible and do not get anything from it. It's because they are simply reading the Logos, which is the written Word of God. They feel that once they have read the written Word that they have all the understanding of the Bible they need. But the written Word is only the beginning. Without the Rhema Word, the written Word would not do you any good.

It's like having a complex piece of equipment or computer program and not having any instructions on how to operate it. But reading and studying the Word of God is like reading the instruction manual that gives instructions on the operation of the equipment or program. When God gives you the Rhema, He reveals to your spirit what the scripture means. Revelation is revealed in the spirit. Again, this is why people who are not born again do not get anything from the Bible. Their spirits are dead to God and cannot receive from Him. However, when you become born-again and take the time to read and study the Word, God reveals to your spirit (not your mind) the spiritual meaning of the scripture or passage.

We said earlier that when we are born again, and we read and study the Word (the Logos) for information or meditation, God reveals to us the revelation (the Rhema) and the application. The Rhema is similar to the application in that it is the revealed Word of God, but it differs slightly.

The difference is that the Rhema is the revealed Word of God (the spiritual meaning of the Word), but the application is how that spiritual meaning specifically applies to your particular situation. This is why it is so important for you to spend personal time in the Word of God and attend church so you can hear the preaching of the Word. There are some people who attend church services 3 to 5 times a week. Some are diligent to not only come to church to hear the Word, but they also watch church on television.

I think church attendance is great. In fact, I encourage Christians to attend church as often as possible, as well as find wholesome and Godly teachings on Christian radio and television. However, it is also essential that you spend personal time in the Word—studying what you heard and learned, and seeking the Lord for the application of how to also apply it to your life. You can listen to sermon messages all day and even all week, but if you do not learn how to effectively apply the messages you hear to your life, they will not do you any good.

For many people, church has simply become another form of entertainment. It's not about going to church to hear a message or Word from God that can change our lives anymore; it's now merely about the excitement and entertainment we get from hearing a good preacher. Most Christians do not take notes, purchase cassette tapes, nor do anything else that will help them to later dissect the message and get an application from God.

I have had the opportunity to preach all around the world. After I have preached or taught the Word of God, I often have people come up to me and tell me that they enjoyed the message and were truly blessed by it. When people tell me that, I sometimes ask them what they received from the message. Believe it or not, only about half of the people can tell me anything they have received from a message they just finished hearing no less than thirty minutes earlier.

I believe that the Lord would be more pleased with a Christian who comes to church once a month and not only hears the preaching of the Word, but also goes home and dissects and studies it to get an application for their life, than someone who attends church every time the church doors are open but never gets any application. If they never get the application, the Word would never become effective in changing their life. I am not saying that we should not attend church; on the contrary. What I am saying is that we should make the effort to get the application of what God is saying to us in His Word so that we will know how to relate it to our lives.

For example: you may read or hear the preacher preach about Samson and Delilah. The Rhema that may come from this account is that we can toy and play with "Spiritual Delilahs" which can hinder or destroy us spiritually just as Delilah did Samson. The application may be to know what specific areas in your life you have been playing and toying with (Delilah's), and the way to avoid them.

The Morning Time — The Right Time

Hast not thou made an hedge about him, and about his house, and about all that he hath on every side? Thou hast blessed the work of his hands, and his substance is increased in the land.

Job 1:10

When we rise early in the morning and enter into prayer and petition God for our daily bread (the things we need), God places His hedge around us. This hedge consists not only of our natural provisions, but also His power, anointing and protection. In the above passage Satan is petitioning God to get to Job's life. He complained to God that there was a hedge around Job's home, family, finances, and all his possessions.

He also complained to God that he could not touch Job's life as a result of this hedge. Job's hedge came as a result of his diligent and disciplined prayer life. As you read the first chapter of Job, you will find that Job prayed for his family daily. This is what kept the devil out of Job's life, and it's the same thing that will keep the devil out of our lives. When you are faithful, disciplined and diligent in prayer to ask for your daily bread, like Job, God not only blesses you with provisions; He also builds up a continual hedge around your life, family and blessings.

> *And in the morning, rising up a great while before day, He went out, and departed into a solitary place, and there prayed.*
>
> **Mark 1:35**

Some people feel that it doesn't matter what time of day you pray just as long as you pray. However, I differ greatly from this belief. I differ from this belief for several reasons: One reason why rising early in the morning is the best time is because there are less distractions. Remember, you are in a spiritual warfare.

The enemy knows that if he can hinder you from praying, that he can also hinder your effectiveness against him. So he does everything he can to keep you from praying. One day you may wake up late in the morning. The next day it may take you a while to find something you need for work. The next day there may be an unusual problem with your children or spouse that needs your attention and takes up your prayer time.

There are all kinds of distractions that can keep you from your prayer time with the Lord in the morning. This is one of the reasons why Jesus rose so early in the morning to pray. He understood His mission, and understood that Satan was going to fight Him every step of the way. And, the only way that He could remain victorious was to pray. If Jesus had waited until later in the morning, the devil would have used someone to distract or hinder Him from prayer. Therefore, He rose early to pray.

The devil will use anyone or anything he can to distract you from prayer. He will use your spouse, children, friends, people calling on the telephone, and an assortment of gimmicks and tactics to keep you from prayer. The people that he uses to distract you do not know that they're being used by the devil. What happens is that the devil puts something into their mind which seems innocent to them—not knowing that they are being used by him to hinder you.

Another reason why the morning time is the right time for prayer is because you are praying for your day. Remember, you are to pray for your **"Daily Bread."** You are to pray for your needs for the day. You are to pray and ask God for His direction, instructions, guidance, protection, safety and other necessities. If you wait until noon or the evening to pray, you would not have properly covered yourself for that morning. You want God's direction, protection and provisions upon your life beginning in the morning, not starting at noon; therefore you must rise early and pray before your day begins.

Distractions of Prayer

Some people do the right thing by praying in the morning, but they attempt to pray while doing other things. If I can use a cliché, they are attempting to "kill two birds with one stone." While this may be a good practice for some things, it is not one that we should use regarding prayer. I have heard of many people who attempt to pray while doing other things such as driving to work in the morning, getting ready for work, and other morning necessities. I am not saying that it is completely wrong or vain to pray while doing these things. In fact, there are times when my available time forces me to do it myself. But what I will say is that this is the wrong priority and pattern for prayer. There will be some days that you may run late for work, and time will necessitate that you use the time you have available to pray. However, this should not be your pattern or practice of prayer.

I used to have an uncanny knack of being able to watch television and talk to my wife at the same time. I could never understand why my wife would wait until I'm glued deep in either one my favorite television shows or the last few moments of a highly exciting sports game, and then want to talk or ask me a question.

My knack was to be able to listen to her while listening to the television at the same time. I could look her in the face while at the same time paying close attention to what was being said on television. Periodically, she would ask me if I was paying attention to what she was saying. Usually I'd always repeat the last line or two, assuring her that I was paying attention. However, even though it looked like I was giving her my attention, I was actually giving my attention to what was on the television. I knew everything that was being said on television, but only paid enough attention to my wife to be able to remember the last statement or two she had made.

One day while I was deep into a sports game on television, my wife asked me a question and I answered her. I guess she was so amazed at my being able to do this that she decided to continue talking. She went on with the conversation for about five minutes. I responded with a casual yes, no, and other comments to assure her that I was listening. She then asked me to tell her what she had said a few moments earlier. Remember, my knack of listening to her while watching television only extended about a sentence or two. So when she asked me what she had said earlier, I was completely dumbfounded. She then discovered my secret. From that point on I could no longer pull that stunt with my wife.

I said all that to say this: although you can give some attention to two completely different things, it is impossible to give your undivided attention to two completely different things. Just as my wife does not like talking to me about something important while I am watching television (because she knows I would be somewhat distracted), I believe that God feels the same way when we pray to Him while we are doing other things.

Now when I say pray to Him, I'm talking about your initial first prayer in the morning. Remember, it's in the morning that you are to begin your day with thanksgiving, praise, and daily petitions with God. This is the time that God wants your undivided attention. He doesn't want to share you with your preparations for work, or dodging cars in traffic while driving to work. He is the King of the universe and the Lord of your life. And, if our spouse (or anyone else) feels it is disrespectful to attempt to converse with them while being attentive to something else, don't you think God would likewise see it as disrespectful to Him?

While you are driving, you must keep your mind somewhat on the traffic. While you are at home preparing for work, you will also become somewhat distracted with morning work preparations (such as looking for things). Although you can pray and prepare for work at the same time, you are going to be distracted, and thus not give God your undivided attention. All through the Bible it talks about praising the Lord and serving Him with all of your heart. You cannot talk to Him, serve Him and worship Him with all of your heart while you are doing other things. So the proper way to pray is to get alone and talk to Him without distractions. Again, there will be days when the lack of time will force you to pray while doing these things (because it's better to pray while doing these things than not to pray at all in the morning), but you should not make it a practice.

Chapter 7

Forgive Us Our Debts

In several Bible translations, the word "debt" is translated to mean, "trespass." Many of us who were taught the Lord's Prayer as children were actually taught to say *"forgive us for our trespasses as we forgive those who trespass against us."* I remember one day looking for this passage (*...forgive us for our trespasses...*) in the Bible, and was disturbed when I could not find it. But I soon discovered that it was simply a translation and not a literal quote.

God has established in His Word laws and commandments for us to follow. Whenever we disobey His Word, laws or commandments, we violate or trespass the laws of God. Whenever there is a trespass or violation of a law, the guilty party who violates the law is indebted to the person, organization, or municipality which they violated. For example, let's say someone named John was driving down a highway, and that portion of the highway had a posted sign for the speed limit of 55 mph. Let's also say that John is like most drivers who sometimes drive above the speed limit. In this example, John was driving 65 mph (speeding) instead of the posted speed limit of 55 mph. While John was speeding, a waiting state trooper clocked his speed and eventually pulled him over. The officer then wrote John a speeding ticket, which is also called a speeding violation. As we all know, whenever we receive a ticket for a violation, there is also a monetary fine that must be paid. When John began speeding, he broke the law and became indebted to that town or city for violating their law. There are many different variations in the amount to be paid for speeding tickets across the country, but there is one thing that is always constant: no matter where there are speeding violations given, there is always a debt (usually monetary) that must be paid.

Once a person has acquired a debt, it must be paid in accordance to the laws and statutes of that jurisdiction. If it's a minor debt such as our example with John speeding, it can be paid by simply paying the monetary fine. Once the fine has been paid, the debt is then canceled. However, there are some criminal acts that can only be paid by serving jail or prison time. Once a person has served their (sentenced) jail or prison time for an offense, it is said that they have paid their debt to society.

Let me first of all reiterate the fact that all of God's laws, instructions and directives in His Word are commandments. Some people think that the 10 Commandments were the only laws given by God. The 10 Commandments were only one set of many laws and commandments given by God in both the Old and New Testaments. Let me also say that there are no big and little sins with God; one sin is just as big as another sin. We have a way of justifying some things we do by attempting to minimize or colorize certain sins. Many people classify sins such as murder and adultery as big sins, while classifying sins such as lying and gossiping as little sins. This classification of sins only works with man. With God, each time we violate His Word (with something we feel to be either a great sin or a little sin), it is the same with Him. Now, just as there is a penalty that must be paid when we violate the laws of man, there is also a wage or penalty that must be paid when we violate the laws of God.

The Penalty Of Breaking The Law

For the wages of sin is death; but the gift of God is eternal life through Jesus Christ our Lord.

Romans 6:23

The wage or penalty for breaking man's laws can (except for malicious murder) either be paid by paying a monetary fine or serving a jail or prison sentence. But unlike breaking man's laws, the above passage shows us the penalty for breaking the laws of God. It is the same penalty for breaking "any" of His laws. It's death! This death is not referring to a natural, physical death, as when a person physically dies; it is referring to a spiritual death.

Know ye not, that to whom ye yield yourselves servants to obey, his servants ye are to whom ye obey; whether of sin unto death, or of obedience unto righteousness?

Romans 6:16

Who knowing the judgment of God, that they which commit such things are worthy of death, not only do the same, but have pleasure in them that do them.

Romans 1:32

He that hath an ear, let him hear what the Spirit saith unto the churches; he that overcometh shall not be hurt of the second death.

Revelation 2:11

There are basically three types of death. One is the physical death as in when a person dies. We will talk more in the next chapter about the second type, which is spiritual death. The three passages above refer to the third type of death that is a spiritual death, which literally means "hell." This death will come after the unrighteous have stood before God and been judged by Him. This is the eternal damnation of hell with all of it's torment. With this understanding, Romans 6:23 can be read like this: *"The wages or penalty of breaking God's laws or commandments is the punishment of eternal hell.* In addition to that, unlike man's laws in which there are different penalties for breaking them, the penalty for breaking any of God's laws is the same—death (hell).

You see, hell was not prepared for man. It was prepared for Satan and all of his followers. However, when Adam sinned, he took on the nature of sin, and likewise the penalty of sin. Whenever a person sins in life, even if it's just one sin, they become indebted to God for breaking His laws, and sentenced to pay their debt of eternal damnation in hell. Some would hear this and say that if this were true (which it is), then there would be no way any of us could avoid hell. After all, the Word of God tells us in Romans 3:23, that *"all have sinned, and come short of the glory of God."*

While this may seem totally unfair to some, it is God's law. But God in His wonderful mercy and grace has made an escape for us. God sent Jesus Christ to die for us. There were three primary purposes for Jesus to come in the earth.

One was to teach us the true love of God, as well as teach us His Word and His ways. The second purpose for Jesus' coming was to successfully live a perfect life in the earth. This glorious accomplishment allowed Jesus to carry out His third reason for coming, which was to take our place and pay our penalty (debt) to the Lord for breaking His laws.

> *... the soul that sinneth, it shall die.*
> **Ezekiel 18:4**

Again, this death is not talking about a physical death, but the eternal death of hell. When God said, *"the soul that sinneth, it shall die"* (suffer punishment), this was a law that could not be changed. The only way for God to prevent His people from facing the penalty of eternal damnation in hell was for someone to pay the penalty for us. The punishment that Jesus took prior to His death was for the penalty of mankind. The cruel, barbaric beatings, torture, punishment, and ultimately being nailed to and dying on the cross was not for Jesus' sins, but ours. He was perfect and had no sins. He paid our penalty for us. He took upon Himself the sins of the world of all those who would accept Him as Lord, and receive Him into their hearts.

Let's use John for an example again. Let's say that John became enraged over a particular incident, got a gun, and killed someone in his anger. At the end of John's trial, the judge and jury found him guilty of murder and sentenced him to the death chamber. Let's also say that our judicial system allowed someone to take John's place in the death chamber. This person willfully volunteered to serve John's time in prison and took his place in the death chamber, allowing John to go free even though he was guilty. This is what happened to us. Jesus took our place. He took our punishment for us. And since the penalty has been paid, our debts of punishment, torment and death have been canceled.

Again, God's law could not be changed. But even though we (those who accept and receive Jesus into their hearts) will not have to pay the penalty of hell for our debts of sin, someone still had to pay it. Jesus paid it for us.

> *For God so loved the world, that He gave His only begotten Son, that whosoever believeth in him should not perish, but have everlasting life.*
> **John 3:16**

Jesus paid the penalty of hell for us — allowing us to go free. All a person has to do to receive this wonderful gift of salvation is to accept Jesus Christ, and truly, intimately receive Him into their heart. Once they do this, they put on the righteousness of Jesus Christ that is without sin, and become worthy of heaven. They do not become worthy because they were perfect or sinless, but because they put on the perfect righteousness of Jesus Christ, and because He paid the penalty for their sins. There are some religions that claim that Christians are too narrow-minded when we say that only those who receive Christ shall have eternal life. God made the laws, not us. Many scriptures tell us that the only way to God is through Jesus Christ. So we must follow His way. People of other religions that do not believe or receive Jesus Christ will have to bear the burden of paying their debt (hell). That's why the Bible says that Jesus is *"the way, the truth, and the light."* I thank God that we have Jesus, who took and paid our penalty.

Now, even though our penalty has been paid, whenever we violate God's laws by sin or disobedience, whether intentional or unintentional, God still requires us to repent or ask for His forgiveness.

Repentance

True repentance is not something that merely comes from our lips, but something that must also come from our hearts. For example, a criminal can get convicted of a crime and be imprisoned. He can feel sorrowful and remorseful about his crime because he had to go to jail, not because the crime itself was wrong. The person who commits fornication and contracts AIDS may be feel sorrowful and remorseful about what they did because they contracted AIDS, not because they committed fornication and sinned against God. Even though they may be sorrowful, it is not true repentance.

True repentance is this:

1. **Thinking Different**
2. **Feeling Different**
3. **Choosing to do Different.**

Thinking Different: This is to have a different attitude about the sin. As we stated above, many people feel sorrowful about their sins only because of the consequences of their sins. It's the consequences that cause many to become sorrowful, not the act of sin itself. Thinking different about sin is to become sorrowful about your sins not only because of the hardship or consequences it may have caused you, but because you realize that you broke the law and commandment of God.

Feeling Different: This is to have a godly regret and sorrow from within.

For godly sorrow worketh repentance to salva-
tion not to be repented of: but the sorrow of the
world worketh death.

2 Corinthians 7:10

This passage shows us what it means to feel different. The sorrow of the world is to only be sorrowful or remorseful based on the consequences. Godly sorrow on the other hand is different. In order for you to have a godly sorrow you must give place to the Holy Spirit to bring conviction upon your heart. There can be no Godly sorrow in a person's heart without the conviction of the Holy Spirit. The Holy Spirit is always knocking at our hearts to show us our sins and bring us to Godly sorrow, which brings about true repentance. But the question is, when the Holy Spirit comes to knock on our hearts, will we receive or ignore His voice?

Wherefore as the Holy Ghost saith, today if ye
will hear His voice, harden not your hearts...

Hebrews 3:7-8

You harden your heart by continually ignoring the voice of God. This is when the Holy Spirit comes to speak to your heart about your wrongs or sins, and you refuse to hear Him speak to you, and you also refuse to receive His correction and repent. When The Holy Spirit comes and speaks to your heart, open your heart to receive Him and His corrections. Do not try to play dodge ball with God by giving a reason or excuse for your sins. Do not try to justify your sins. Let the Holy Spirit speak to your heart. Be open to His correction, and be quick to repent.

If a person sins against God and there is no inward, Godly sorrow of their heart, then that person has not truly repented. God not only looks upon the outward appearance (words from their lips), He also looks on the inward part (the inward condition of their heart regarding their sins and repentance).

Choosing to do Different: This is the third thing that must take place in order for repentance to be true and authentic. If a person does not choose to go in a different direction after they have sinned, they will continue to go in the same path and thereby make the same mistakes—continuing to sin. If you accidentally placed your hand on a hot stove and burned your hand, you would change your course of actions to make sure that whenever you came near that stove in the future, you would not make the same mistake and burn your hand again. If you fall into sin, you should do the same thing. Pray and ask God to help you to take a different course of action regarding your sin or temptation. Whenever someone falls into sin, it is always a path that led them there. Choosing to do different is to pray that the Lord will help you to choose a different path, and thereby avoid making that mistake again.

Daily Repentance

Repentance is not something we do once a month when we take communion; nor is it something we only do after we have committed what we call, "the big sins." Remember, everything Jesus instructed us to do in this outline of the Lord's Prayer is something that we are to pray for or pray about every day. So when Jesus instructed us to pray and ask the Lord to forgive us of our debts or sins, He was instructing us to repent every day.

Search me, O God, and know my heart: try me,
and know my thoughts: and see if there be any
wicked way in me...

Psalms 139:23-24

In this passage David asked the Lord to search him to see if there was anything that was wicked or evil in him. Whenever we truly ask the Lord to search us, He will always show us areas of our lives in which we need to repent and change. It may not be anything serious at that time. It may be something that is somewhat minor. However, the Bible tells us in Song of Songs 2:15, *"it's the little foxes that spoil the vine."* In other words, the (so called) big sins do not begin as big sins; they begin as little sins.

It's the (so called) small, insignificant sins we don't think are serious that eventually lead to our demise in what we call big sins. For example: The sin of adultery could have begun by watching a television program that was too seductive. The sins of lying, gossip, or even anger could have come from watching soap operas or not properly praying.

One of the ways in which Satan gets strongholds in our lives is through unrepented sin. When you enter into your prayer time and devotion with the Lord each morning, ask the Lord to search your heart about sins you may have committed the previous day. As the Lord shows them to you, be quick to repent of them. Again, it doesn't have to be a big sin. It could be something little (little foxes) such as not praying and touching the face of God like you should have. It could also be something such as you telling a lie, gossiping, lusting or any number of sins. Whatever they are (large or small), ask the Lord to search your heart and show them to you. This kind of daily repentance will keep Satan from using the little foxes to get a stronghold in your life.

Like David, we should ask the Lord to search our hearts each day. And, when we ask the Lord to search our hearts, He will always show us something. When you repent of the little foxes, it keeps the devil from causing them to grow into strongholds.

Know That God Is Faithful To Forgive You

If we confess our sins, He is faithful and just to forgive us our sins, and to cleanse us from all unrighteousness...

1 John 1:9-10

...if any man sin, we have an advocate with the Father, Jesus Christ the righteous: And He is the propitiation for our sins: and not for ours only, but also for the sins of the whole world.

1 John 2:1-2

Some people think or feel that certain sins are too serious for God to forgive them. Others feel that their sins are too numerous for God to forgive them. But we must understand that the same blood Jesus shed on the cross forgives all of our sins regardless of how great or small the sin, or how many times we have committed the sin. The only thing God is looking for is for you to have a true heart regarding your repentance (to think different about that sin, to feel different about it, and to make an attempt and choose to do different or choose another path).

If you have truly repented of your sins, you can come before God boldly knowing that He has forgiven you and has cleansed you with His precious blood. Don't listen to the devil when he tells you that you're not forgiven because your sins are either too great or numerous. Listen to God's Word when He tells you that when you repent (true repentance), you are forgiven.

Repentance is a good thing, not a bad thing. I repent every day of something. The things that I repent of may be small and insignificant to some, but I am open and willing for the Holy Spirit to bring the little things to my heart so that I may repent of them and get the help of the Holy Spirit, rather than wait until they become big sins, whereby I need deliverance.

When the scripture says, "Forgive us our debts," it is saying that we should honestly and openly "daily" ask the Holy Spirit to search our hearts for sin and disobedience, and be quick to repent of them, allowing God to cleanse us of our sins and bring us deliverance.

Chapter 8

As We Forgive Our Debtors

W e talked earlier about how merciful God was to send Jesus Christ for us to take our place and pay the price for our sins. And, when we sin against God, all we have to do is be open and honest with Him, and truly repent, and He will forgive us. However, all that is tied up into this part of that passage, *"as we forgive our debtors."* God ties or connects our forgiveness with us forgiving others. Let's look at a parable that Jesus gave us that correlates this point:

> *Therefore is the kingdom of heaven likened unto a certain king, which would take account of his servants. And when he had begun to reckon, one was brought unto him, which owed him ten thousand talents. But forasmuch as he had not to pay, his lord commanded him to be sold, and his wife, and children, and all that he had, and payment to be made. The servant therefore fell down, and worshipped him, saying, Lord, have patience with me,*

and I will pay thee all. Then the lord of that servant was moved with compassion, and loosed him, and forgave him the debt. But the same servant went out, and found one of his fellowservants, which owed him an hundred pence: and he laid hands on him, and took him by the throat, saying, pay me that thou owest. And his fellowservant fell down at his feet, and besought him, saying, have patience with me, and I will pay thee all. And he would not: but went and cast him into prison, till he should pay the debt. So when his fellowservants saw what was done, they were very sorry, and came and told unto their lord all that was done. Then his lord, after that he had called him, said unto him, O thou wicked servant, I forgave thee all that debt, because thou desiredst me: Shouldest not thou also have had compassion on thy fellowservant, even as I had pity on thee? And his lord was wroth, and delivered him to the tormentors, till he should pay all that was due unto him. So likewise shall my heavenly Father do also unto you, if ye from your hearts forgive not every one his brother their trespasses.

Matthew 18:23-35

The above parable is a clear example of what I am saying. The one man asked the king to forgive him of his debts. The king in his mercy forgave him, but the same man refused to forgive someone else who was indebted to him. After the king found out, he had the man put in prison.

God commands us to forgive others who have wronged us in order for us to receive His forgiveness. I can understand how difficult it can be to forgive some people who may have severely hurt or disappointed you. I had a brother who was dear to my heart to be maliciously murdered. I was a new Christian at that time. Up until that point I had found it easy to forgive people of things such as lying on me or talking about me behind my back, but the murder of my brother was a completely different thing. After the funeral, I prayed and said that I forgave this person, but later found that I still held it in my heart. Sometimes a person can be offended to such a degree that it takes more than simply saying that they forgive them.

Sometimes you have to actually work on it. You have to work on it because some offenses hurt you down to the core of your heart. It's like scrap metal or a bullet that has been imbedded deep within you, that cannot simply be scraped off your skin, but must be surgically removed. I found that in order for me to really forgive this person, I had to begin praying for them.

> *Bless them that curse you, and pray for them which despitefully use you.*
>
> *Luke 6:28*

When you pray for someone, prayer pulls down the walls of division, anger, and unforgiveness—which enables you to not only forgive them with words from your lips, but to also truly forgive them in your heart.

When you find it difficult to forgive someone, you need to work on it by praying for them at least once a week, and even more if necessary. This is what I had to do for the person who killed my brother. I had to keep them lifted up in prayer. I not only prayed for their forgiveness, but I also prayed for their salvation, and for the Lord's blessings and mercy to be upon them. It actually took me several months after I began praying for them before I could honestly say that I had forgiven them in my heart.

This is not something that you will want to do or feel like doing, but rather something you need to do. It's like dieting or exercising. Your body does not want to diet or exercise, but you make yourself do it because you know that it is good for your body. Likewise, your mind and heart will not want to pray for a person who has severely hurt, disappointed or offended you. They may be the last person in the world you may want to pray for, but you do it anyway because you know you must do it in order to truly release them from your heart.

The Bondage of Unforgiveness

When Jesus said for us to pray for those who despitefully use (or offend) us, most people think that Jesus was instructing us to do this only to be kind and forgiving. However, this directive is actually more for our benefit than the person who may have offended us.

> *Therefore if thou bring thy gift to the altar, and there rememberest that thy brother hath ought against thee; leave there thy gift before the altar, and go thy way; first be reconciled to thy brother, and then come and offer thy gift.*
>
> *Matthew 5:23-24*

When you harbor unforgiveness in your heart, it becomes an open door for Satan to not only come in your life, but to also hinder your prayers. Unforgiveness is part of a group of sins that Satan uses in the form of witchcraft. As long as you are operating in this form of witchcraft (unforgiveness), it hinders your prayers. The above passage validates this point.

The alter represents a place of prayer, and the gifts represent your praise, worship and petitions. God is saying that when you know there is either anger, unforgiveness or strife between you and your brother (this also includes your spouse), do not even try to come to God in prayer until you have made an attempt to make it right with them. I specify "making an attempt" because some people may not be willing to talk to you about the offense or reconcile their differences. But when you make the (honest and sincere) attempt to reconcile the situation (even if they do not want to do it), you are then released (in the spiritual realm) from the spiritual hindrance and bondage of the offense.

Unforgiveness brings everyone connected to it into bondage. It brings the one who made the offense into the bondage of being indebted to the person whom they offended. It brings the person who was offended into the bondage of anger and gives Satan an open door to come in other areas of their life. And, it brings both parties into the bondage of having their prayers hindered.

You cannot truly pray or worship the Lord with anger, unforgiveness or strife upon your heart. You can go through the motions of trying to talk to God, but you will soon find that when these things are harbored in your heart, the door is shut. Once you either make it right or make the attempt to make it right, the door is then opened.

So forgiveness is not something you do simply to be kind or to show how mature of a Christian you are, it's also something you do because you understand the spiritual implications it can also have on hindering your prayers and your life.

Think About Your Sins

If you still have difficulty forgiving someone who has offended you, then do this: Begin to think about some of the hideous sins you have done in your life. You know, the kind you haven't told anyone about, and the kind you are ashamed of and hope no one ever finds out. Yes, those kind. Imagine yourself standing before God, and God tells you that because you received Jesus Christ into your heart, that Jesus paid the price for your sins and all of your sins are forgiven except a few of them. And, the only reason why you are not being forgiven for them is because you failed to forgive people who offended you. And, because you now have to pay the penalty for these sins, instead of you spending eternity in heaven with God, you will spend eternity in hell paying your debt for your sins.

This is a frightening thought—or at least should be. There have been people who have severely offended me in life since the murder of my brother. Some of them have been just as hard to forgive as it was for the murderer of my brother. But when I thought about having to spend eternity in hell paying the penalty for my sins because I would not forgive them, I had a much easier time forgiving them.

Like the parable we read earlier, you cannot expect God to be merciful to you if you are not willing to be merciful to others. The choice is yours. You can either hold on to your offenses and harbor anger, strife and bitterness against people who have offended you and let them take you to hell, or you can release forgiveness to them, thereby allowing the blood of Jesus Christ to cleanse your sins and spend eternity in heaven. Again, the choice is yours.

Chapter 9

And Lead Us Not Into Temptation

Some people hear this passage and take it to say that God is saying that we should pray that He would not lead us into temptation. Some people think that God tests them with temptation to see whether or not they will stand. But the truth of the matter is that God does not tempt us at all.

> *Let no man say when he is tempted, I am tempted of God: for God cannot be tempted with evil, neither tempteth He any man.*
>
> **James 1:13**

This passage validates the point that God cannot be tempted with temptation Himself, and neither does He bring temptation upon any person. So then, why does the scripture tell us to pray, "*...Lead us not into temptation?*" This passage is not instructing us to ask God not to lead us into temptation, but rather, to pray that we would not yield to the path of temptation. A paraphrased version of this passage would

read, *"and lead us away from the path of temptation."*
Again, you are not to pray that God would not tempt you,
but to pray that He would give you the strength, mind and
will to "not" yield to it, and resist it instead.

Drawn Away By Our Own Lusts

But every man is tempted, when he is drawn away
of his own lust, and enticed.

James 1:14

When the scripture says that we are drawn away of our
"own lusts," it is referring to those things that individually
and personally tempt and entice us. Just as we are all made
up differently, we all also have different things that tempt
and entice us.

There are different body features that entice a person to
the opposite sex. To some, it's the color or shade of their
skin; to others, it's their physique; and to another, their
beauty or handsomeness is the only thing that matters. This
same principal can apply to just about any area of life.

There are some people who have either never taken
drugs, or only briefly experimented with them at a young
influential age. But the same ones who have never had a
bout with drugs may have struggled at some phase in life
with alcohol, smoking, or with some other substance abuse.
You can even find people who have never struggled with
substance abuse, but have had bouts with sin in other areas.
Some may not commit adultery or fornication, or may not
have even been addicted to a substance, but their struggle
may be the sins of lying, gossip, backbiting or slander. As the
phrase goes, "different strokes for different folks." It's something different that draws or entices each one of us to sin.
This is why Jesus instructed us not to look down upon or

belittle someone who is struggling in a particular area. Because even though you may not be struggling in that area, you may have just as bad of a struggle in another area.

> *And why beholdest thou the mote that is in thy brother's eye, but considerest not the beam that is in thine own eye? Or how wilt thou say to thy brother, let me pull out the mote out of thine eye; and, behold, a beam is in thine own eye? Thou hypocrite, first cast out the beam out of thine own eye; and then shalt thou see clearly to cast out the mote out of thy brother's eye.*
>
> *Matthew 7:3-5*

One person's "own lusts" may not be the same as another person's own lusts, but they could still be just as bad. Jesus lets us know that we are hypocrites when we have issues in our own lives and look down at someone else's issues that may be different from ours.

When Temptation Becomes Sin

QUESTION: When does temptation actually become sin?

> *Then when lust hath conceived, it bringeth forth sin..."*
>
> *James 1:15a*

To answer this question you must first understand that the battlefield of sin and temptation is the mind. It's in the mind that the devil tempts, tests and tries us with temptation. The sin does not come merely because you have been given an evil or sinful thought. When Jesus was tempted in the wilderness by Satan, He was given the thought to commit sin, but

He didn't yield to it. The question is this: If the sin doesn't take place when we get the thought, when does it take place?

The sin actually takes place when you give conception to it. It's like when a woman conceives a child. Conception takes place when the sperm of a man joins together with the egg of the woman. Once this takes place, it forms what is called an embryo. The embryo is actually the beginning of conception. In the same manner, the sin comes when sinful conception takes place. It's when Satan gives you the thought, and you receive it in your heart. While it (the thought) is in your mind, it is only temptation at that point. But the moment you take the thought is when you give conception to it and it becomes sin. Taking a thought is to receive the thought into your heart, make up in your mind to do it, or make plans or purpose in your heart to carry it out. Jesus shows us this same principle in the following passage:

> *Ye have heard that it was said by them of old time,*
> *thou shalt not commit adultery: But I say unto*
> *you, that whosoever looketh on a woman to lust*
> *after her hath committed adultery with her already*
> *in his heart.*
>
> *Matthew 5:27-28*

Prior to this point, the Jews believed that they only committed adultery when they physically carried out the act. But Jesus brings clarification to this sin by letting them know that adultery begins when they conceived the sin of lust in their heart. This same principle works no matter what area it may be. If Satan tempts you to tell a lie, the sin (of lying) does not begin when you physically tell the lie, but rather, when you receive the temptation in your heart to lie, and make up in your mind and heart that you are going to tell it.

The Death of Sin

QUESTION: Is there a difference between conceiving a sin into your heart and physically carrying it out?

The answer is "YES." There is a difference between conceiving the thought of sin from Satan and physically carrying out that thought.

> *Then when lust hath conceived, it bringeth forth sin: and sin, when it is finished, bringeth forth death.*
>
> *James 1:15*

The difference is that when you conceive a sin in your heart, you have already sinned against the Lord and are indebted to Him for that sin. However, when you physically carry it out, there is another level of spiritual destruction that goes along with that sin. It's death!

In our previous chapter, we discovered that there are two kinds of death. We all know about the first kind of death, which is a physical death, as in when a person dies. We also discovered that there is another kind of death, which is a sentence of hell. But this passage above refers to a third kind of death. This kind of death is a type of separation from God. This is the same kind of death Adam experienced when he sinned against God.

> *And the LORD God commanded the man, saying, of every tree of the garden thou mayest freely eat: But of the tree of the knowledge of good and evil, thou shalt not eat of it: for in the day that thou eatest thereof thou shalt surely die.*
>
> *Genesis 2:16-17*

Some people (who do not know how to rightfully divide the Word of God) would look at this passage and say that God lied. They would say that God told Adam that he would die the day he disobeyed God. Adam didn't die a physical death the day he sinned against God because he lived hundreds of years after his disobedience. He didn't die the type of death of hell as talked about in our previous chapter on that day; so what kind of death was God referring to? He was referring to a third kind of death, which is a separation from God.

Adam initially had a continual, ongoing commune and relationship with God. He also walked in divine authority with God. But the very day (as God had instructed) that he sinned against Him, he was cut off from his intimate place, commune, and position with God. Even though Adam was eventually able to still pray to God, and on occasion have fellowship with Him, it was nothing like his original position and place with Him. Each time we disobey and sin against God, we go through a little more of a death. Sin separates us farther and farther from the Lord.

Romans 8:35, asks, **"What shall separate us from the love of God."** It's not that God separates Himself from us; sin separates us from God. Sin even separated God from Jesus Christ His Son for a moment. When Jesus hung on the cross, God took all the sins of the world—past, present and future, and placed them on Jesus. When this was done, Jesus experienced a separation from God for the first time in His existence. This is when Jesus cried out on the cross, *"My God, My God, why hast thou forsaken me?"* It wasn't that God had forsaken or abandoned Jesus; God simply cannot stand the presence of sin and had to separate Himself from Jesus while the weight of the sins of the world hung on Him. When we sin, we allow the weight of sin to separate us from God. So when the scripture says, *"...and sin, when it is finished,*

bringeth forth death, it is talking about the slow death or separation from God.

When you become separated from God you get to a place where you can't sense His presence, hear His voice, feel His power or anointing, or experience the true place of intimacy with Him like you once could. This type of death can be a slow process, which is why many people never realize that they have experienced this death until it has caused dramatic changes in their life. The scripture in James 1:15 tells us that this kind of death takes place when the sin has been carried out. Some believe that when they conceive a particular sin in their heart, they might as well carry it out. They believe this based upon the fact that they know that when you sin in your heart that it is still a sin with God whether you carry it out or not. But the act of carrying out a particular sin has further consequences—spiritual death.

Another biblical term for this type of death is called backsliding. When we say that a person has backslidden, what instantly comes to our minds is someone who has begun drinking, taking drugs, committing adultery or fornication or other types of sins. Although these types of sins can become manifestations of backsliding, backsliding itself begins far before these acts ever take place. It's when you allow sin to separate you from the conviction and fear of God and you step back from Him.

Backsliding begins when Satan continually comes and tempts you, and even though you hear the voice of the Holy Spirit attempting to get you to resist Satan and not yield to his temptation or sin, because of your "*own lusts*" and undisciplined inert desires, you continually ignore the voice of God and give in to temptation or sin. Each time you do this, it's like you have taken another step away from God. If you were to take a step backwards, you would still be close to your original position. However, if you took one step away from that position each day, after a month or so you would find yourself far away from your original position. This is what backsliding is like. It's a little by little step away from God that begins when you take that first step. It's not that God has left you; you allow your (continual) sins to cause you to step away from God.

> *Now the Spirit speaketh expressly, that in the latter times some shall depart from the faith, giving heed to seducing spirits, and doctrines of devils; speaking lies in hypocrisy; <u>having their conscience seared with a hot iron</u>.*
>
> **1 Timothy 4:1-2**

To have your conscience seared with a hot iron is like taking a wrinkled shirt and ironing over the wrinkles until they are gone. The wrinkles represent the fear, conviction, and voice of God. When you sin against God, the Holy Spirit will begin speaking to you about your sin and attempt to bring conviction upon your heart. But the more you ignore His voice, it's like you ironing the wrinkles out of the shirt. If you keep ironing it, soon there will not be any wrinkles left. Likewise, if you keep resisting the voice and conviction of the Holy Spirit, soon you won't hear His voice or feel His conviction at all. This is the type of death that James 1:15 is talking about when it says, *and sin, when it is finished, bringeth forth death.*

The only thing that eradicates this type of death or separation is true repentance. It's the kind of repentance that we discussed earlier. Remember, we said that true repentance is thinking different, feeling different, and choosing to do different. True repentance closes the gap of separation and brings us back from this spiritual death to life with God.

Chapter 10

And Deliver Us
From Evil

In the book of Judges you find the children of Israel going through seven cycles of sin. First, they would leave God and begin to walk in sins and abominations. Next, because of their sins and abominations, God would take His hands off of them, allowing their enemies to come and overtake or capture them. Then, because of their oppression, they would repent of their sins and begin to cry out to God for His help and deliverance. In His mercy, God would then send them a deliverer (such as Gideon and Samson) who would help to liberate them from their oppressors. After a while, they would soon forget about how they were under oppression and bondage, and how they cried out to God, and He delivered them. They would then go right back into sin and begin the cycle all over again. This cycle happened seven times with seven deliverers in the book of Judges.

This cycle of sin for Israel represents the same cycle of sin that many Christians go through. Some spend their entire Christian lives experiencing defeat after defeat going through the same cycle. We all know that God is a merciful God, and He will forgive us for our sins when we cry out to Him from a true and sincere heart. But after God has forgiven us, He doesn't want us to stop there at forgiveness, but take a step further and seek deliverance so that we won't have to continue to go through the same cycle of sin (such as Israel did in the book of Judges). Look at the pattern in which God is leading us in regarding our sins:

1. Forgive us for our debts (sins)
2. Lead us not into temptations
3. Deliver us from evil

First, you are to ask for God's forgiveness for the sins you've committed. Next, pray that He would give you the mind, will and strength to resist the devil and not yield to temptation. And finally, if you do yield to temptation, seek deliverance from it. The purpose of seeking deliverance from your sins is to keep you from going through (like the children of Israel) the same cycle of sin over and over again. Seeking God for deliverance keeps you from continually going through this redundant cycle.

The Blame Game

Deliverance begins when you stop making excuses for your sins and blaming other things for causing you to sin. We live in a society that blames other things and people for our failures in life. No one is to blame for their sins or crimes anymore. It's always the parents, their upbringing, their environment, their economic status, or any number of things other than themselves. This evasion tactic has even rubbed off on the church. We too have entered into the blame game.

> *And the LORD God called unto Adam, and said unto him, Where art thou? And he said, I heard thy voice in the garden, and I was afraid, because I was naked; and I hid myself. And He said, Who told thee that thou wast naked? Hast thou eaten of the tree, whereof I commanded thee that thou shouldest not eat? And the man said, The woman whom thou gavest to be with me, she gave me of the tree, and I did eat. And the LORD God said unto the woman, What is this that thou hast done? And the woman said, The serpent beguiled me, and I did eat.*
>
> *Genesis 3:9-13*

The above passage is the account of Adam and Eve directly following their disobedience after being beguiled by Satan. First, God asks Adam about his sin. Instead of him taking responsibility for his actions, he blamed the woman. When God asked Eve, she blamed the serpent. But God didn't buy into this blame game. He dealt with each of them. When the Holy Spirit comes knocking upon your heart about your sins, don't try to play the blame game with God, go ahead and acknowledge your sins. When you acknowledge your sins to God and take responsibility for them, you are now on your way to receiving deliverance.

Realize You Need Deliverance

If you want deliverance, you must become open and naked before God about your sins and your spiritual condition. When people begin programs such as AA (alcoholics anonymous) or DA (drugs anonymous) meeting, the first thing they must do is acknowledge that they are an addict. Before you can ever get deliverance from anything, you must first acknowledge where you are.

When I was in the military, I found that for me, one of the most difficult things to do was to navigate or find my way around in the woods. It was even more difficult in the deserts. When you are out in the woods or in the desert, everything looks alike, so it is very easy to get lost. It seemed that for a while, getting lost was a daily undertaking for me. Eventually I became better at reading a map and using a compass and didn't get lost as much. And when I did, I learned how to navigate my way to where I needed to be. I learned that the first thing I needed to do was realize I was lost. I can't tell you the number of times I stood up in my vehicle and said to myself, "I have no idea where I am." Once I realized I was lost, I had to get my map and compass and find my location. Once I found my location, I could then navigate my way back on course.

It's the same in the spiritual realm. Until you come to the realization that you need help and deliverance, you can wander aimlessly in spiritual circles for months, years or even decades. In the parable of the prodigal son, the son had to come to himself before he could find his way back to the father. It's the same with us. You must realize and acknowledge to God that you need help and deliverance in order to get it.

You may need deliverance and not realize you need it. We can easily see someone who is bound by alcohol, drugs, pornography, or some other type of addiction and see that they need deliverance. Although you may not need deliverance in any of these areas, there may be areas in your life where you do. Your area of deliverance may not be one of these, but it could be pride, gossip, backbiting, lying, overeating, or any number of other things. Before you look down at others, ask the Holy Spirit to check your heart to see if there is an area in your life where you need deliverance.

Once you realize you need help, you must then become open and honest with God about your sins and transgressions. He already knows what you've done. He was there when you did it, and saw the intentions and motives of your heart when you did it. So since He knows it all, you might as well get honest with Him anyway. It's one thing to repent of your sins, and it's another thing to know you need help and deliverance from them. Once you have recognized where you are, and the fact that you need deliverance, you are on your way to being spiritually liberated.

Never Accept Defeat

There are some Christians who become entrapped in a particular web of sin so long and so often, that they actually begin to accept this position of spiritual bondage and defeat. Some not only accept this position of defeat, they even come to enjoy it and even love this position. Sometimes the struggle to get deliverance becomes so cumbersome that it may seem easier to just accept this position of defeat than to keep fighting it. You must make up in your mind to never accept defeat.

> *I returned, and saw under the sun, that the race is not to the swift, nor the battle to the strong...*
> **Ecclesiastes 9:11**

> *...but He that endureth to the end shall be saved.*
> **Matthew 10:22**

These two passages are often quoted as one scripture, when in fact they are two separate scriptures. However, although they are separate, I believe that they go together in understanding. When you put these two passages together, you come up with this understanding: The race of heaven (and your deliverance) is not given to the one that can begin the fastest or be the most impressive, but to the one who can continue to endure. Endurance and persistence is the key to your deliverance.

Whether you have fallen one time or hundreds of times, don't stop and give up. Get back up and get back in the race. The trick of the devil is to get you to feel that you will never get deliverance over certain problems and sinful habits in your life, thereby getting you to accept this position of spiritual defeat. Tell the devil he is a liar! Tell him you are never going to give up or give in, and that you will get your deliverance! The key is to keep fighting. It doesn't matter how many times you have fallen in the mud and slime of sin, get back up and repent (from your heart) and get back in the race. And, if you are a fighter and never give up, you will eventually get the deliverance you desire.

Resisting The Enemy

Some try to resist Satan solely on the strength of their will. There are areas in each of our lives where it doesn't take much effort to resist the devil. While on the other hand, there are other areas in which we are strongly drawn or tempted. There is however, a strong caution I would like to give about relying on your own will to resist the devil. The caution is that Satan comes against us in waves. He will war against you for a season in a particular area, then he will leave you for a while, and eventually come back and hit you in that area later.

> *And when the devil had ended all the temptation, he departed from Him for a season.*
>
> Luke 4:13

This passage comes after the temptation of Jesus in the wilderness. Notice, it says that the devil departed Him for a season. In other words, the fierce spiritual fighting of temptation was over for a while. The danger for us is to think that just because the primary wave of fighting is over, that we have completely conquered the situation. When people think they have spiritually conquered a situation, they have a way of letting their guard down. Then after a season, (while their guard is down) the enemy will sneak back in and hit them with another fierce attack and overtake them.

This is why you should never become comfortable depending upon your sheer will to resist the devil alone. Your sheer will can only carry you so far. But, if you depend upon the Lord to help you, deliver you, and give you the strength to resist the devil, His strength will take you through.

> *And lest I should be exalted above measure through the abundance of the revelations, there was given to me a thorn in the flesh, the messenger of Satan to buffet me, lest I should be exalted above measure. For this thing I besought the Lord thrice, that it might depart from me. And He said unto me, My grace is sufficient for thee: for my strength is made perfect in weakness. Most gladly therefore will I rather glory in my infirmities,*

that the power of Christ may rest upon me.
                                    2 Corinthians 12:7-9

In this passage Paul deeply sought the Lord three times for deliverance from a particular issue. We do not know what particular issue or area of his life that he sought the Lord for deliverance. It could have been a particular trouble, sickness or temptation. The particular situation is not as important as the fact that he sought the Lord, and the answer in which God gave him. God's answer was, *"My grace is sufficient for thee: for my strength is made perfect in weakness."* In other words God was telling Paul that He was not going to launch Paul out of the situation, but, if he (Paul) would rely on the Lord for His (the Lord's) strength, that He (God) would strengthen him, help him, and take him through his particular crisis.

Walking in your own strength to resist the devil will cause you to walk in vain pride, and will eventually lead you to failure. But if you learn to lean and rely on the Lord for His strength, He will take you through.

Watch And Pray

One thing that you must remember about getting deliverance is that if you have ever fallen into a stronghold, you have the propensity to possibly fall into that snare again. It's like an alcoholic or drug addict. Once they have been delivered, they must always be on the lookout for the possibility and danger of slipping back into that trap again. They cannot go to bars, or hang around people or atmospheres that would be conducive to leading them back into their addiction. They must stay away from those areas as much as possible. Likewise, in the spiritual realm, once you have come under bondage in a particular area, you must always be mindful of the fact that you can come under bondage again.

This is why when you ask the Lord for His help, you never stop praying and depending upon Him to not only help you, but to also keep you. After you have sought Him diligently to get your initial deliverance, you must also continually seek Him in order to keep your deliverance and victory.

Let's take for example a man who has fallen into fornication or adultery. First, the conviction of the Holy Spirit comes over his heart which brings him to repentance. After he has repented, he must then seek the Lord in prayer, asking the Lord to deliver him from the spiritual bondage that has griped his heart. Then, he must continue to seek the Lord and never stop seeking Him for His continued deliverance.

When you repent and seek God for deliverance, He delivers you from the snare of the enemy. However, because Satan once obtained a grip on you in that particular area, it allows him access to easily bring you back under bondage in that area again through temptation and seduction. Therefore, you are not to give the devil any place in your life.

The way you keep from giving him place in your life is to stay in prayer and continue to confess the Word of God over this area. While there is still a strong pull of temptation in this area, pray and confess the Word of God over this area every day, and if needful, several times a day. Once you are sure that you have obtained victory in this area, you should still pray about it and confess the Word of God over it at least once or twice a week. This is how you keep from giving the devil place in that area.

Take The Full Prescription

I want to use a medical example of what happens if you do not continue in prayer and confessions. Let's say a person became infected with strep throat. When they visited the doctor, the doctor would prescribe them some type of antibiotic for the infection. When a doctor prescribes an antibiotic, they usually tell the patient to take the antibiotic for the full 10-day period.

When the patient gets home and begins taking the antibiotic, the symptoms usually begin subsiding in about a day or two. Then in about three to four days the symptoms usually completely disappear. The patient feels fine at this time and believes that it is okay to discontinue taking the antibiotic. Then after about a week's time the symptoms they had of strep throat begin to reappear, except this time it's worse than it was originally. The person must then go back to the doctor to be retreated.

Once the doctor reexamines them and finds that they are still infected with strep throat, they always ask the question, "Did you take the medication for the full 10 days?" Of course the answer is always no. The doctor then instructs them specifically to go home and take the medication for the full 10-day prescribed time. Whenever they take the medication for the full amount of time prescribed, the infection becomes completely eradicated.

Let's look at what happened medically: When a person has become infected with strep throat, this means that infectious bacteria have overcome the person's immune system and infiltrated that particular area. When the doctor prescribes the antibiotic and the person begins taking it, the antibiotic helps the body's immune system to fight off the infectious bacteria. When this begins, the person starts to feel better. When 70-80% of the infectious bacteria are destroyed, the patient usually does not feel any more symptoms. However, once they stop taking the antibiotic, it allows the small residue of the infectious bacteria the opportunity to build itself up again. Then, before long, the person has the same problem they had originally. Had they taken the medication for the full 10 days as prescribed, it would have given the antibiotic a chance to completely eradicate the infectious bacteria, thereby not giving it a chance to come back again.

This medical process is an example of the way sin and strongholds work in our lives. Once the devil has obtained a stronghold on an area in your life, it's equivalent to a person getting strep throat. Repenting and seeking the face of God is the equivalent of taking the antibiotic for the first three or four days.

Even though they feel good, and feel like they have been delivered (like the remaining infectious bacteria), the devil is always lurking around for an opportunity to get back in. The way that you keep him out is to continue to take the medication of prayer and confession of God's Word. But what's different is that you never stop taking your medication.

> *When the unclean spirit is gone out of a man, he walketh through dry places, seeking rest, and findeth none. Then he saith, I will return into my house from whence I came out; and when he is come, he findeth it empty, swept, and garnished. Then goeth he, and taketh with himself seven other spirits more wicked than himself, and they enter in and dwell there: and the last state of that man is worse than the first...*
>
> *Matthew 12:43-45*

This passage is a spiritual principle of the medical example given earlier. It reiterates the point that once you have repented and sought the face of the Lord for deliverance, Satan is always lurking about, looking for an opportunity to get back in. In this passage, it says that when Satan comes back after he has been cast out, he finds the place is empty, swept and cleaned. This represents how that a person can repent and get cleansed of the sin. But if they do not fill that (now empty) place with the presence of God through prayer and confession of His Word, then Satan can come in again. The key to getting your deliverance is (true) repentance. But the key to keeping your deliverance is to keep your house (your spirit) filled with God's presence and the anointing by praying and confessing His Word.

If you do not already have it, I highly encourage you to get our book, *"The Weapons of Our Warfare, Volume III."* It explains in detail what confessions are, the necessity of confessions, how they apply to our lives, how they build us up, and how they help us in praying.

Whatever It Takes

The points we have discussed thus far are things that will help you to get deliverance. However, you can only get deliverance to the degree that you truly want to be delivered, and are willing to do whatever it takes to get your deliverance. In Isaiah 1:19, it tells us that we must be *"willing and obedient,"* meaning that you must not only have a desire to be delivered, but you must also be willing to do what God has instructed you to do in order to get your deliverance. In James 2:20, it says, *"faith without works is dead."* This means that you can have faith in a particular thing all day long, but until you put forth some effort in that thing, the promise of that desire will die (never come to pass).

For example, if someone was unemployed and wanted to get a job, they can pray, confess the Word, and release faith all day and night, but they will never get that job until they put forth some action and get up and go out there and begin to look for that job. God will open the doors for us, but He will not pick us up from our bed and take us to the door. We must want it, and be willing to do something to get it. God is a God of action. He requires some action on our part. If you notice, most of the time that Jesus healed someone, He had them to do something. He didn't need them to do the things they did to receive the miracle, but by them doing so, their faith became ignited and put in a position to receive the miracle. Just as action was required for them to receive their miracle, action is also required for us to receive our deliverance.

Deliverance is different for every person and for every offense. When you seek the face of God for deliverance, the Holy Spirit will begin teaching you what you need to do in order for you to keep your deliverance. But again, you must be willing to do whatever it takes to get it.

> *Is not this the fast that I have chosen? To loose the bands of wickedness, to undo the heavy burdens, and to let the oppressed go free, and that ye break every yoke?*
>
> *Isaiah 58:6*

Many times your deliverance will begin with fasting. Some people can get their deliverance if they can just break the stronghold. Fasting does just that; it helps you to break the stronghold and addiction of sin. For some, God may simply require you to go on an initial fast to break the stronghold grip of sin. For others, God may require you to go on a continual fast once a week or once a month to maintain your deliverance. It's different with everyone, but the Holy Spirit will direct you.

* **NOTE**: There are different types of fasts. Please get our book, *"The Warfare of Fasting"* to find more about fasting, different types of fasts, its effectiveness in our spiritual lives, and how fasting helps to destroy the yokes of the devil.

Give No Place To The Devil

Give no place to the devil (Paraphrased).
Ephesians 4:27

Sometimes it's not so much that the devil has overcome us, as much as the fact that we have given him a place to overcome us by putting ourselves in a position to do so. If you really want deliverance, you must stop giving him place in your life, by closing the door that has given or is giving him access to your life.

Television and Movies

Sometimes closing the door may require you to stop yourself from watching certain kinds of television shows or movies. It is said that television and movies are our biggest influence to sin. Some people actually receive their deliverance, but allow the wrong (negative influential) movies or television programs to bring them back into bondage.

As you seek the Holy Spirit for your deliverance, ask the Lord if there are any movies or shows you have been watching that have influenced you in that area. If there are, and you truly want deliverance, the Holy Spirit will definitely show them to you. You must then discipline yourself not to watch them. Prohibiting yourself from watching these shows may be difficult, but you can do it. If God reveals to you that this is the case, pray and ask Him to help you to overcome the lure to watch them and He will help you.

Internet Websites

The same can be said about certain internet websites. Although the computer can a be a very powerful resource for knowledge and information, it can also be a stumbling block for drawing you to certain ungodly websites. You can now literally find anything on the internet. And, you don't necessarily have to be looking for something ungodly to find it. It comes looking for you through seductive instant messages, seductive and ungodly chat rooms, and unsolicited pornographic email and web links. The internet has become a demonic stronghold for many men as well as women of God.

If you have become seduced by it, I recommend installing some kind of parental firewall. It will not block out all of these types of sites, but it will greatly help reduce them. I also recommend that you discipline yourself not to use the internet at times that may be more tempting for you to visit these types of websites, such as late at night after everyone has gone to bed.

Music:

Certain kinds of music can be just as seductive and luring. Many Christians only look at the lyrics in a song to
judge whether they are something they should or should
not listen to. Sometimes there is a spiritual influence behind the music.

> *And it came to pass, as we went to prayer, a cer-*
> *tain damsel possessed with a spirit of divination*
> *met us, which brought her masters much gain by*
> *soothsaying: The same followed Paul and us, and*
> *cried, saying, these men are the servants of the*
> *most high God, which show unto us the way of*
> *salvation. And this did she many days. But Paul,*
> *being grieved, turned and said to the spirit, I com-*
> *mand thee in the name of Jesus Christ to come out*
> *of her. And he came out the same hour.*
>
> *Acts 16:16-18*

In the above passage, this woman was possessed with a
spirit of divination (fortune teller) and followed Paul and
other apostles everywhere they went saying, *"These men*
are the servants of the most high God, which show unto us
the way of salvation." On the surface there seemed to be
nothing wrong with what this woman was saying. But
Paul eventually became grieved in his spirit with this
woman and her saying. Paul finally realized that this
woman had an evil spirit upon her, which probably had
been hindering them in their work for God. After realizing
that she had an evil spirit upon her, Paul cast it out of her.

Likewise, as a Christian, you must realize that there are
sometimes evil spirits behind things that seem to be innocent. Whether it's movies, music, television shows or any

number of things, you must learn to judge these things by the spirit, and not simply by thier exterior appearance.

People:

We've talked about television shows, movies, websites, and music, but another influence that we may have to give up is the negative influence of people. There may be some people in your life that may be destroying your spiritual walk of victory. Friends, relatives and peers can influence you like nothing else. Sometimes you have to even give up your common relationship with certain people if you want to get true deliverance. This was Samson's problem with Delilah. He thought that he could handle her influence and bring her over. Instead, her influence destroyed his testimony, and almost destroyed him.

We talk about Samson and how he was influenced and deceived by Delilah, but the question is, what kind of Delilahs are you messing with? A Delilah could be your best friend you've known for years. They may be some of your co-workers, or even some of your family members or relatives. They could even be some of your church members. Satan will use whomever he can to keep you from your victory in Christ.

Sometimes we can know that a person is a negative influence upon us, but we talk ourselves into believing that we can change them. And, instead of us changing them, their influence actually keeps us from walking in victory. Pray and ask the Lord to show you those around you who are a negative influence upon you. Once the Lord shows them to you, it sometimes becomes necessary to just let them go. When I say let them go, I'm not saying that you should completely cut off your communication and relationship with them, but you may need to taper it some. You can still talk with them about general things, but you need to be bold, take a bold stand for Christ, and let them know that you are a Christian, and you don't do certain things anymore. Hopefully this should cause them to begin to respect you and not try to entice you to ungodly things and conversations. If it doesn't, you then need to begin tapering off some of your social fellowship with them.

These are just a few areas of our lives in which we give the devil place to hinder us and keep us in bondage. There can be many other areas. The thing to do is to continually pray and ask the Lord to show you these areas. Once He shows them to you, you must be willing to cut them off.

> *If thy right eye offend thee, pluck it out, and cast it from thee: for it is profitable for thee that one of thy members should perish, and not that thy whole body should be cast into hell. And if thy right hand offend thee, cut it off, and cast it from thee: for it is profitable for thee that one of thy members should perish, and not that thy whole body should be cast into hell.*
>
> *Matthew 5:28-30*

It is obvious that Jesus is not talking about literally cutting off your arm or hand, or cutting out your eye. He is referring to cutting off the access to whatever has been luring and drawing you to sin and temptation. In other words, it is better to do without watching certain television shows or movies, and without surfing the internet, listening to certain kinds of music, going to certain places, or keeping close relationships with people that have a negative influence upon your life. It is better to keep away from these things or people, than to allow them to continue to keep you in spiritual bondage all of your life and possibly take you to hell.

Get the Power You Need

But ye shall receive power, after that the Holy Ghost is come upon you: and ye shall be witnesses unto me both in Jerusalem, and in all Judea, and in Samaria, and unto the uttermost part of the earth.

Acts 1:8

Behold, I give unto you power to tread on serpents and scorpions, and over all the power of the enemy...

Luke 10:19

If you want to walk in the power of God, you need the Baptism of the Holy Ghost. There is a difference between being born-again, and being filled with the Holy Ghost. When you become born-again, you receive a measure of God's spirit within you. But when you get filled with the Holy Ghost, you receive the fullness of His power that helps give you the power to resist Satan and his demonic temptations and strongholds. The Holy Ghost is not reserved for any special group of religious fanatics, or for those with a special call of God. It's reserved for everyone. All you have to do is to want it and ask God for it. Having the power of the Holy Ghost will make the difference in your life. If your church does not believe in receiving the Baptism with the Holy Ghost, seek the Lord about talking to someone who can help give you an understanding of it, and how to receive it.

Getting More Spiritual Fuel

I've been asked this question: If being baptized with the Holy Ghost gives you all this power, why is it then that you hear of so many people who are supposedly filled with the Holy Ghost falling into sin? My answer to that is twofold: As we discussed earlier, you must want to be delivered. You must make up in your mind that you don't want to be under the bondage of sin, and that you are willing to fight and do whatever it takes to obtain and keep your liberty in Christ. We discussed earlier that we all have our "own lusts." They are things that personally and individually draw us. These people do not have a true drive and desire to fight against the enemy. They have negotiated a spiritual truce with the devil in this area and have given up.

The second part of my answer to this question is that they probably need to get more fuel. Let me use an analogy to explain what I mean. Before you become born again, it's the equivalence to riding a bicycle. After you become born again, it's like you go from riding a bicycle to driving a small car like a Geo Metro. This car is one of the smallest cars made on the road. It doesn't have much luxury in it and neither does it have much power; however, it is far better than walking or riding a bicycle.

After you receive the Baptism with the Holy Ghost, it's like you go from having a small 100 Horsepower Geo Metro to driving a powerful 320 horsepower Hummer. The Hummer is one of the most powerful vehicles on the road. It's the same vehicle used by the military. Anyone who has owned a big powerful SUV knows that it takes a lot of fuel to operate and move such big engines and vehicles. Now even though the Hummer is a powerful vehicle, if you do not put any fuel in it, it will be worthless to you and of no more use to you than a bicycle.

> **And be not drunk with wine, wherein is excess; but be filled with the Spirit.**
>
> *Ephesians 5:18*

Many people see this passage and think that it is saying that we should not drink wine. There are other scriptures that relate more directly to drinking wine. This passage is not referring to drinking wine, but rather, comparing the influence of wine to the influence of the Holy Spirit. It is telling us that instead of being under the influence of wine, to seek to be filled with the Spirit of God and operate under His influence instead. Notice, it tells us to *"be filled,"* meaning that we have the ability to be filled. Having the Baptism with the Holy Ghost gives you the vehicle or power to resist the devil and overcome his temptations and strongholds; however (like having a high powered Hummer), you must make sure you have fuel (be filled with His spirit) in order to operate and utilize that power.

People who have received the Baptism with the Holy Ghost and still walk in sin are people who either do not want to fight and resist the devil, or they do not put any fuel in their vehicle. Again, God gives us the powerful vehicle (like the Hummer) of the Holy Ghost, but it's up to us to get a fill up. When we run low on fuel (even though we have a spiritually powerful vehicle), we put ourselves in a position to fall into the temptations, seductions and strongholds of the devil. But when we put fuel in our vehicle (become filled with His Spirit), we have the ability to overcome all of Satan's temptations, strongholds and seductions.

Chapter 11

For Thine is the Kingdom, the Power, and the Glory, Forever

I am Alpha and Omega, the beginning and the ending, saith the Lord, which is, and which was, and which is to come, the Almighty.

Revelation 1:8

God is the all powerful, all knowing, omnipotent and sovereign God. Everything begins with God, and everything also ends with Him. As we discussed earlier, when we enter into prayer, we enter by giving God praise, worship, adoration and thanksgiving. Likewise, when we end our prayer, we should not simply end with our relentless petitions, but by giving God worship, praise, adoration and exaltation again. When I say enter into prayer, I'm not talking about the regular times of the day in which we talk to God, but rather, our first time of the day in which we enter into His presence.

We discussed that there is a correct way in which you enter into the throne of God. There is not only a correct way that you are to enter into the throne of God, there is also a correct way you are to exit the throne of God. And, just as improperly entering into prayer can result in you not getting your prayers answered, improperly exiting prayer can also result in you not getting your prayers answered.

When you end your prayer, spend a few moments exalting God. Tell him how great He is and how good He is. Tell Him how powerful, mighty and magnificent He is. Tell Him how much you adore Him and appreciate Him being your God. Give Him all the glory and praise He deserves. You may have prayed for thirty minutes to an hour, but this part only takes a few moments.

When you end your prayer, you should not only end it with praise, exaltation and adoration, you should also end with thanksgiving. There's a song that came out years ago called, "Don't wait 'til the battle is over, you can shout now!" This song makes the same point we are making here. If you have a crisis in your life and you have prayed about it, and God answered your prayer and delivered you, you would give God praise and thanksgiving. Because you've prayed in faith, and you know that God has heard you and will deliver you, you don't have to wait until you see the manifestation; you can go ahead and give Him praise and thanksgiving for it now, because it is on the way.

Let's say that you applied for a mortgage for a new home. Let's say that you have picked out your dream home. You love it and you are in high anticipation for an answer from the mortgage company about either your approval or disapproval. When would you begin your celebration of victory? Would you begin your celebration when you received word from the mortgage company that your loan had been approved? Now certainly you would really celebrate after you have physically moved in your house, but the celebration would begin when you were told that your loan was approved and it was yours. Likewise in prayer, when you have prayed and petitioned God for something, end your prayer by not only giving Him the praise, worship and adoration He deserves, but also end it by giving Him thanksgiving for answering your prayer. Because, by faith, it's already done. After you have properly given God the praise, worship, adoration and thanksgiving, you can then properly exit or end your prayer.

I encourage you to read this book over and over again. If there are areas in your prayer life that are still lacking, pray that the Lord would give you the mind, strength and will to fulfill His Word and instructions concerning the basics of prayer. After you have become disciplined in these principles of prayer, I encourage you to go to the next level. Our next book will be entitled, "Standing in the Gap." This book will take you beyond the basics of prayer and into the next level of intercession.

Other Books and Materials
By Kenneth Scott

The Weapons Of Our Warfare, Volume 1
This is a handbook of scriptural based prayers for just about every need in your life. There are prayers for your home, marriage, family and many personal issues that we face in our lives each day. If you desire to be developed in prayer, then this is a must book for you.

The Weapons Of Our Warfare, Volume 2
This is a sequel of Volume 1, and brings the prayer warrior into the ministry of intercession. It has prayers for your church, pastor, city, our nation, and many other national issues in which we should pray for. If you desire to be developed as an intercessor, then this book is for you.

The Weapons Of Our Warfare, Volume 3
(Confessing God's Word Over Your Life)
There is a difference between prayer and confession. This book gives the believer understanding about confessions and what they do in your life. It also contains daily confessions for major areas of your life. If you have Volumes 1 & 2, then you also need Volume 3.

The Weapons Of Our Warfare, Volume 4
(Prayers for Teens and Young Adults)
Teenagers have different needs than adults. This is a prayer handbook that keeps the same fervency and fire as Volumes 1 & 2, but also addresses the needs of teens. This book is a "must" for your teens.

The Weapons Of Our Warfare Volumes 1 & 2 on CD
Meditate on the Word of God as it is prayed on audio CDs. These CDs contain prayers from Volumes 1 & 2 (sold separately). As you hear these prayers prayed, you can stand in the spirit of agreement and apply them in the spirit to your life, situations and circumstances as you ride in your car, or as you sit in your home. These CDs are a must for every Christian library.

The Weapons Of Our Warfare Volume 3 on CD
This CD series contains the same confessions that are in "The Weapons of Our Warfare, Volume 3." In this series Pastor Scott will lead you in confessions, allowing you to easily follow and quote them afterwards. Make confessions of the Word of God throughout your day as you sit at home or drive in your car.

When All Hell Breaks Loose

Most mature Christians can survive a casual trial here and there, but many of God's people fall during the storms of life. Get this book and learn how to prevail through the storm *"When all Hell Breaks Loose."*

Praying in Your Divine Authority

Many Christians are hindered and defeated by Satan simply because they do not know the dominion and authority they have in Christ. This book teaches the believer how to bind and loose Satan and demon spirits, and how to pray and walk in our divine authority.

The Warfare of Fasting

In Matthew 27:14 Jesus said that some spiritual strongholds, hindrances and bondages will only be broken through prayer and fasting. This book teaches the believer the different types of fasts, the methods of fasting, and the warfare of what happens in the spiritual realm when we fast. If you want to see "total" deliverance in your life, you need to get this book.

Standing In The Gap

In this book Pastor Scott teaches life-changing principles of what it means to make up the hedge, stand in the gap, stand in agreement, and intercede for others. If you are a prayer warrior, an intercessor, or you have a desire to be one, this book is a "must" for you.

Chains That Bind Generations

Do generational curses actually exist? Where do they come from? Does God send generational curses upon my life, or are they from the devil? Could it be that some of my difficulties and struggles in life come from generational curses? If there is a curse on my life or family, can it be broken? Using the life of David, Pastor Scott answers these and other questions about generational curses and teaches you how to get set free and receive your deliverance from generational curses.

The Witchcraft of Profanity

When people use profanity, they think they are speaking empty, vain words. These words are not vain at all. Each of these profane words are actually witchcraft spells, evoking specific demon spirits which come to hinder and destroy specific areas of their life and the lives of those they speak over. Get this book and learn what's actually going on in the spiritual realm when profanity is used. Once you read this book, you will never use profanity again.

For inspiring CD messages and other available materials, visit us on the web at www.prayerwarfare.com

Contact Us:

For prayer requests, questions or comments, write to:

Spiritual Warfare Ministries
Attention: Kenneth Scott
P.O. Box 2024
Birmingham, Alabama 35201-2024

(205) 853-9509

<u>Web Site:</u>
www.spiritualwarfare.cc
or
www.prayerwarfare.com

email us at sprwarfare@aol.com

This book is not available in all bookstores. To order additional copies of this book, please send $10.99 plus $2.98 shipping and handling to the above address.

God has anointed Pastor Scott to teach and preach on the power of prayer. If you are interested in him coming to minister at your church or organization, please contact him at the information above.